MW01107754

Built Like a Woman

DEDICATION
To Angus

Built Like a Woman

Sandra Broman

Illustrated by Richard Baxter

MURDOCH BOOKS

contents

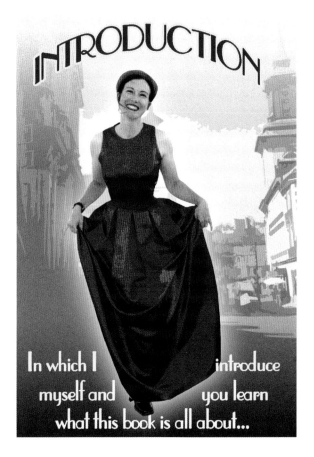

1

INTRODUCTION

In which I introduce myself and you learn what this book is all about...

This book contains all I know about life surrounding building and renovating—from a woman's perspective. If you are already working on your dream home or are filled with longing for the day when you will be ankle deep in mud with a cement root perm, this book is for you. If you are being patronized or disregarded simply because of your gender when visiting the hardware store, then this book is also for you. After you have finished reading it, I hope you will have gained confidence, inspiration and some practical advice.

I was once told on the phone that my timber merchants didn't want to speak to me after they had delivered some wood that was definitely not what I'd ordered. They insisted they would only speak to my builder (which also happened to be me) as I kept asking stupid questions. I didn't think my questions were stupid at all. Frustrated, I ended up getting a professional carpenter to look at my pile of timber, call the merchants on my behalf and ask the same stupid questions. The next day they delivered what they should have delivered in the first place, and as a bonus let me keep the wrong stuff free of charge. Perhaps they hadn't wanted to listen to me because I kept referring to the wall plate as the 'bit of timber that goes on top of the wall' and the purlins as 'the bits that go across the roof'—'your terminology is wrong, love'. So, for your enlightenment I have included a section on how to sound like you are wearing stubbies.

This basic approach to the art of building is continued throughout the book. When explaining things—from how to prevent chilblains to coping with on-site stress—I am assuming you have no prior knowledge. Maybe you already know more about cooking without a kitchen or on-site safety than I do, but this book is aimed to give confidence to the absolute beginner, as well as offering support to the rest of you!

I used to be hopelessly inept at DIY. After a harrowing experience doing woodwork in school I learnt to hate it. I felt threatened by all the whizzing and whirling of drills and saws. When I first started doing things to my house I would handsaw everything and make little crosses anywhere I wanted a drill hole. I would then wait for my husband to come home and do the actual drilling for me. But that's not really DIY, it's more like SEDI (Someone Else Does It)! After a while I thought it was also truly pathetic— what could possibly be so scary about drilling? So, after desperately waiting for the Drill Man to come home one day, I picked up the drill and just…did it. That was one of the defining moments in my life. My newfound skill made me so happy that I went out and bought a power saw. Over the years I have gradually reduced my fear of using tools until this year I bought the scariest tool of all: a chainsaw. If I can do it, so can you!

EARLY INSPIRATION

I grew up in a 1960s house on the Swedish west coast, born of two parents who didn't have a handy bone between them. They loved looking at old houses but wouldn't live in one as the constant upkeep that kind of house requires would have been an almost impossible burden for two people so disinterested in renovation work. Long summers were spent at my grandmother's summerhouse. She owned a pretty wooden house teetering on the edge of grey granite cliffs strewn with purple heather and dark green pines, permanently hunched over from the wind. The yellow-painted house bordered the blue-grey sparkling fjord, creating a veritable visual feast. I loved everything about it: the sloping floors, the furniture, the little yellow bowls she served berries in, the salty smell of the sea that permeated everything, the tiny playhouse and equally minuscule guesthouse. I was blessed with so much as a child to inspire me as an adult. Everyone is, I suppose, it just comes in different guises.

Look to your childhood for things that made deep impressions on you. You will find plenty of inspiration to draw on for your own home.

As a girl I dreamt of old houses. Apart from owning a dog and a horse, to live in an old house was what I wanted most of all. My family would spend weeks every summer travelling around Europe, looking at art and architecture. While my friends went skiing or to the beach, we looked at old churches and Frans Hals paintings. I imagined myself living in some of the houses we visited. I drew plans of how I would furnish them. Sometimes a quick glimpse of a house exterior or the feel of a certain village was all that I needed to inspire me. Especially charming were the narrow Dutch houses, filled with that special Dutch sense of cosiness. The narrow, winding stone pathways of the Greek islands enthralled me as a teenager, and the sight of a medieval stone wall proudly rising out of the mists still makes me go all weak. From very early on I had an obsession with living environments.

As an adult, a friend convinced me to go with her to Australia. I reluctantly agreed, but had no real desire to go there. What did Australia have to offer me? Not having visited before, I imagined it to be unnecessarily hot and dusty, with too much space, no old houses to admire, and just a bunch of flea-bitten kangaroos jumping across a road shimmering with heat, all ringed by a too big and too wet shark-filled ocean. Anyway, we went and Australia turned out to be a very friendly and relaxed sort of a place with delicious cool drinks and perfectly good coffees waiting for me in little cafes, absolutely huge skies of liquid gold everywhere I cared to look, and quite a few old houses. After a couple of weeks, I met an Australian and didn't go home again for over two years. Then we went to Sweden together with the intention of living there, as I'd become homesick. I found I was missing the cold dark winters, illuminated by endless candles and smelling of wet wool. I wanted to wrap myself in the soft summers, full of vigorous greenery and flowers and very unthreatening—barely any snakes at all…

But, after only a year in Sweden we flew back. Perhaps it was because the approaching winter dark didn't appeal as much as I'd thought, perhaps because of how noticeably polluted Europe is when you've been away for a while, perhaps because it was my husband's turn to contract a spot of homesickness. I can't really remember the actual reason. But we returned, and the sun again shone hotly on our heads while snakes frolicked with the numbats in the bushes.

THE FIRST PROJECT

We decided to move to South Australia, as the real estate in this region was still affordable. A year after our arrival I fell pregnant and had a baby boy. I had found a turn-of-the-century stone workers' cottage near the city and told my husband (and the bank) that we were buying it. It was affordable, had potential and we could easily ride our bikes to town. I don't think I fully understood what I was letting myself in for, as it needed a great deal of work. Instead, I was just happy visualizing what it would look like after I'd had my way with it.

This is what you would have seen if you'd been helping us carry boxes on moving-in day in 1991. As a welcome mat, the entire garden space was covered in cracked concrete with a concrete tub containing a dead palm. There was a huge buckled corrugated tin shed covering half of the rear block. The street boundary was defined by one of those really ugly low iron 1970s front fences, with matching curly iron veranda posts, painted a flaky beige. The front door was a hideous modern style that didn't go with the house. Some windows were cracked. The floor inside was chipboard sheeting. On the plus side, the walls were built from bluestone, plastered on the inside. All interior walls were good and free from cracking, had new wiring and fresh pink-painted plaster. There were no interior doors, skirting boards or any other woodwork. The brick fireplaces had been boarded up. There was only a hint of a kitchen, consisting of some ripped-off tiles and a couple of old pipes poking through the wall in the old lean-to that really was leaning. The bathroom consisted of a toilet and a bathtub in an airy enclosure surrounded by building plastic. Half the tin roof looked like it might be the old original, which would need replacing in the near future. My dream home!

The style of cottage was exactly what we wanted; we just couldn't afford anything in better condition. The real estate advertisement described it as a 'renovator's delight', which really meant that it required lots of bloody hard work. It had a Housing Improvement Order on it, indicating there were some faults that needed rectifying before it could be rented out. I remember the order stated it to be 'unfit for human habitation'. I quite liked that, as it appealed to my hitherto little-used pioneering spirit. On the plus side, the foundations were solid and the salt damp was limited to two small places. Beneath the chipboard lurked some gorgeous old pine flooring only slightly cupped, and behind the boarded-up fireplaces hid some old still-working chimney openings. Nothing could dampen my enthusiasm. I ached with desire to turn this little house into the object of beauty it deserved to be. It was to be a great training ground for me.

Now, please understand that I had *absolutely no practical experience at all*. In my past I had hung some pictures using a hammer, but that was about it.

To this day, I have never changed a fuse or washer or repaired a bike puncture and I don't know how to. I never even used to put air in pushbike tyres myself and I only learnt how to check the oil in my car a couple of years ago. I'm ashamed to say it, but those things were *guy* things. So, for my first renovation, I figured I would simply have to work things out as I went along, using books.

The equipment we owned when moving into the house was the following:

◆ one electric drill (which I couldn't and wouldn't use due to a deep-seated fear of electric tools)

◆ one packet assorted drill bits

◆ one screwdriver set

◆ one chipped chisel

◆ one hammer

◆ one handsaw, tenon style

◆ one handsaw, musical style

◆ one handsaw, scroll style, totally useless.

However, I didn't even stop to think I was ill equipped, as I was drunk on hope and joy. It wasn't the prospect of doing the renovation that acted as a stimulant, it was the burning desire to own and live in a beautiful old house. I wasn't planning on doing it all myself anyway, I was going to subcontract so everything would be easy. Perhaps I would paint the walls and sand the floors myself. My husband had made it clear that he wasn't interested in the renovating, but I was happy to do it. After all, he worked full-time, and I was going to be home every day with our son Angus for the first 12 months.

So we moved in. I remember going to sleep the first night. Our bed was temporarily put in the ramshackle lean-to, which was so unsteady it had timber props preventing it from collapsing. That night it rained and I awoke to the surreal feeling of having a fine mist of water settling on everything,

as the old tin roof turned out to be nothing but a giant sieve. Yet, all I could feel was an insane exhilarating joy. What did it matter, that section was getting demolished anyway. The bed got moved in a hurry though…

The first thing I did was to borrow a crowbar from a friend. Armed with that, I felt very handy as I prized up the chipboard from the floor, revealing 100-year-old boards underneath. I wondered why the old owner had gone to the effort of putting the chipboard down; he must have been planning carpets. I tried to sand them using a small electric hand sander, also borrowed, but quickly came to the realization that hiring a large drum sander was better as it ripped into the floors, levelling every last blemish. So far this was all easy work and very encouraging, as the end result was fast and excellent. I repaired a few damaged patches and varnished the floors until they shone almost brighter than my eyes.

As I was at home with the baby, we experienced a bit of poverty as we had only one income, a mortgage and were trying to fix up the house at the same time. All the grand things I wanted to achieve amounted to far more money than we had available. As I got quotes from tradesmen this became painfully obvious. The extension called for a brick wall on the boundary, so I took the cheapest quote out of my three and ended up with a terrible job. It was so dodgy I might as well have done it myself. Then I took the advice of someone we sort of knew and hired a carpenter who unfortunately turned out to have a drinking problem that created all kinds of complications for us. I didn't have the confidence to fire him and take over myself. My plumber killed himself (yes, really true) halfway through the job, though I don't think that was my fault. We were left with no kitchen, no bathroom and only a garden tap on the side of the house to supply all our water. Tradesmen don't like to take over a job someone else has started so in the end I had to get someone straight out of plumber's school to finish the work. As a result of these experiences, I quickly realized that it was going to be so much easier and cheaper if I did most things myself that I simply *had* to acquire the necessary skills. Gradually I tackled bigger and more involved jobs. My confidence boomed and I felt great. It wasn't so hard after all!

SECOND TIME AROUND

Three years after commencing the renovation we put the house on the market. I was getting bored, the house and garden were looking brilliant and I needed a new challenge. My husband liked animals and I liked distance from neighbours so we considered buying some land. He would be able to play with the geese or whatever while I tackled some serious construction. After all, I had now acquired some pretty useful skills and a few more tools. We received just enough money from the sale of our renovated house to pay off the bank and buy a slice of gorgeous Barossa Valley land, plus put a minimum deposit on a tiny seaside investment unit where we could live for a while. With hindsight I realize my husband was quite upset at selling the house, but he did what I wanted without voicing his concerns. He liked comfort and tidiness, yet here I was planning for us to be uncomfortable, primitive and messy for several years! Warning bells ought to have been pealing loud and clear, but like a wombat with a goal in sight I put my head down and ran towards it, with little regard for my surroundings.

The land we bought was on a very pretty hillside on the edge of a little village. There were views all the way to the next town, taking in a panorama of vineyards and groves of trees over which the cockatoos soared. The land came with a shed containing an ancient blue tractor and a collection of rats on one side, and a grove of ancient gnarled almond trees in the middle. There was a dirt track going halfway up the hill, and that was it.

This time, I knew a lot about renovating but neither of us knew anything about looking after land. Big mistake. You have to keep the grass down, and for that you either need livestock or machinery. Whichever path you choose requires work and care. Some months later the grass was so long that four-year-old Angus ventured into it and got lost. The grass was so tall that we could put a mob of sheep in the paddock and not see them for weeks. We were simply not rural folk. Good intentions are insufficient for survival in the country. You need knowledge and experience and that only comes with time. We actually bought a couple of sheep once—retired ones from the local petting zoo—and they told us one was a ewe and the other a ram.

Great, we were going to bring little lambs into the world! However, nothing happened. The mystery was explained when the farmer who took them to be shorn pinned a note to the wool bags when he returned them saying, 'You can't start a breeding program with two wethers.' For those of you even more ignorant than I was, a wether is a neutered male.

MY LIFE AS A BUILDER

I started my construction with a small building on the land. It was a trial run, as I thought a normal-sized house would be the same thing, only on a larger scale. I chose to build a 6 x 4.5 metre (20 x 15 foot) building, approved as a 'garage' by the council—the title 'dummy run' probably would have raised some eyebrows. It was going to be constructed out of rendered concrete blocks. The dirt track had been gravelled and power had been laid on to the site at great expense, I had bought a couple of old doors and windows, a concrete slab was curing, it was all waiting for me to begin.

I was fortunate enough to have a stone mason friend who donated a day of his to give me a crash course in 'How to Lay Blocks'. He came with his dog, Jack, and a picnic basket. It was an icy June morning requiring double layers of clothing, but as the sun grew stronger we peeled off a layer. For me, it was a magical day as we shared sardines, halva and squares of bitter chocolate with Jack on a makeshift lunch setting made from concrete blocks. My friend ran through everything I would need to know in order to put up the walls, and helped me lay the first couple of courses. By the end of the day I felt confident enough to do my wombat imitation and forge ahead on my own.

I had two weeks' holiday during which I planned to get the walls up ready for roofing. We lived 80 minutes away, and every morning I got up while it was still dark, had a big warming breakfast, then drove up and spent the whole day building. When it got too dark to adequately see the spirit level I would stack the next day's blocks (concrete blocks were pale enough to see if there was any moon or, if not, my car's spotlight would provide illumination), so when I returned in the morning I could just get straight on with the job.

Sometimes I'd stop at the local pub on the way back and have a warming drink by the fire, dreaming of the time I could call myself a local and not have to drive over an hour to get home. Then I'd make my way home, aching all over and feeling great. Once there I would have the weirdest bath you can imagine. The shower in our little unit had a deep square base you could plug up; it was a bit like a bath more suitable for washing your dog in. It was around 40 centimetres (16 inches) deep, and just big enough to fit half of me if I folded myself up. If I lay on a diagonal I could submerge my bone-tired back, while I raised my legs vertically up the shower wall. I would alternate this position with sitting and warming my legs.

After two weeks of this routine the walls were up. The only problem now was that we were almost broke, as the building kitty only contained enough for part of the roof. The sale of the tractor—that we didn't want anyway—raised sufficient money to finish the little room. We now had a room to come up and sleep in and store things in, and confirmation for me that yes, I could truly do it. All up, the little yellow house cost $10,000 to build, and was the best thing I could have done. Now all I needed was more money and a cunning plan…

MY OBSESSION DEVELOPS

I have always been arty, but as my skills with tools increased I started making objects from wood and metal and made money from exhibiting in a gallery. The building plans were taking an absolute eternity to be drawn and approved so I needed to keep doing things to increase and maintain my skills as we plodded on, saving money for construction. I also spent lots of time collecting and preparing old doors and windows, acquired from second-hand building supplies and garage sales. In addition, I painted several ceiling murals on masonite. I did a few Renaissance-inspired ones, based on designs I found in a book on old Swedish interiors. Another mural was inspired by the walls and ceiling in a Danish church that I had become besotted with and taken a lot of photographs of. People sometimes ask if that one is 'finished', but we can't all share the same taste… When I was

busily and happily painting my ceiling roses while still living in a unit I'm sure people thought I was jumping the gun a little, but it certainly sustained my morale and meant I was still doing something useful.

When the plans finally came through, I could hardly believe it. Because of being rejected twice before I had almost reached the point of giving up. I had no initial contractors lined up and it was six months before any of the ones I found became free. By then we had managed to save almost $30,000—nowhere near what you need to finish a house with, but enough to start. After that was used up, things would take care of themselves, more money would steadily trickle in, and I would progress building slowly.

I began with the earthworks, hiring men with big machines to cut out an enormous wedge of hillside, and to carve a slowly winding road to reach the house site. Never did I imagine the scarring and damage to the landscape this would create. I got a shock the first time I saw it from a distance, fully realizing the extent of the dent I had caused. I was on my way up a neighbouring hill when something caught my eye. It was my site, making me stare in absolute dismay, knees trembling. What had I done! The site looked like an open-cut mine. However, after about a year, the wound was healing fine.

After the earthworks came the pool. It was the last thing I wanted to spend money on at this early stage, but the way the plan was designed meant that it simply had to be the first thing to go in. Otherwise it wouldn't be possible to have one at all. I wanted a very small pool, just deep enough to swim in, 2.5 metres (8 feet) wide and maybe 5 metres (16 feet) long. I planned to enclose it in a conservatory later. There were several reasons for wanting it to be small: my limited water supply (I collect all I use from the roof), the ease of solar heating it, cheaper to tile, fewer chemicals and less maintenance. We would still be able to swim, as it would have two jets installed at one end to swim against. Not having any idea about how horribly expensive this sort of thing would be, I got disappointed as I called around for quotes. 'All right,' I said to myself, 'I'll delete the pool.' But then I realized that if I started deleting things I passionately desired this early—and something I couldn't reconsider later—why was I bothering with building at all? So I made a firm

decision to go ahead and ignore the expense. My rationale was that I would save a fortune doing things myself and would find more money later on. I'm glad I made that decision now.

What I had now was a gravel road leading to a flat plateau, carved into the hillside. In the middle of this was an incongruously empty concrete pool shell. The next step was the foundations. I had chosen a concrete slab for several reasons. Firstly, because I like it; secondly, because it's good bushfire prevention as sparks can't go under the house; and thirdly, because it offers good thermal value. There was just enough money left to pay for the concrete, the electrician, and the plumber's initial work.

> If you have one really strong idea, don't lose sight of it. Get rid of other, less essential ideas. Remember the thing that got you inspired in the first place. Occasionally, disregard the expense.

Still there was nothing much I could do myself, except for poking around the earthworks picking out rocks that I could use for garden walls afterwards. My own real work would soon begin, and I was busy lifting weights in anticipation. Our finances were less than fine and after buying a semitrailer worth of bricks all the money had run dry. That didn't worry me though, as I knew we could save more while I laid the bricks.

I was having a sterling time, laying brick after brick in the first section of the house. It was Easter school holidays, and every day dawned clear and sunny. The walls grew quickly; they almost went up by themselves. I couldn't stop— as long as the weather held I was there, up to my armpits in mud. By June the roof went on, and by early August we were living in the first section, which included a glazed veranda, one large room and a bathroom. This section was designed to become a B&B later (later is still to come). We split the room up into a tiny kitchen area, two bed areas, and a living area. We bought a couple of kilos of extension cords to enable all these 'rooms' to have power. In the future, the room would only need three double power points but now it needed heaps. The kitchen area had a power board that

overloaded if you used the kettle at the same time as the microwave, so we put the kettle by the bed, as the bedside light didn't have that effect. When the alarm went off in the morning I let my arm fall on the kettle button, and I only got out of bed when the water boiled. I miss that!

Finishing this section cost a lot so there was no hot water on tap until just before Christmas, as we had to save for the solar system. But there was a tiled bathroom with real drains—you just had to heat the water by different means. Luxury! The Christmas school holidays I spent collecting rocks and building terraces on the hillside, which I then filled with soil. This was not exactly needed at this time but it allowed a little money to build up again while I was kept busy doing something that was free. We were pretty comfortable where we were, or at least I was. Angus didn't complain at all. I would have loved to give him a room to himself but happily he was too young to mind. There was always the little experimental building down the drive to go to, which we used as our television room for a while.

I continued on like this, making money and spending it at a fairly even rate. The rest of the house grew and grew. By the time we had lived in the first section for a year and a half, and before the major expense of the roof on the main house had come, my husband and I split up. Financially it was frightening, as I was now a single parent, with a child in a private school, and a low income on which to complete the still unroofed building. I had $20,000 in the bank and was forced to succumb to borrowing money, after pigheadedly refusing to get into debt for so many years. My three-year building permit had only one year left on it and I wasn't able to accumulate money anywhere near as quickly on one income as we had on two. The old car died at the same time and needed replacing. It wasn't the best of times financially. I borrowed some money from the bank and some from my kind and generous parents, and put the roof on.

A lawyer recommended I put a halt to all work, as increasing the value on the property would give more money to my husband in a financial settlement. After all, I was putting all *my* time and money into it. However, I felt stopping was not an option. I was simply in too deep. The house had

become an extension of self and represented years of time spent either thinking about it or working on it. The thought that I might lose it was intolerable. My husband, fortunately, agreed with me and let me keep it.

I found solace in hard work after the initial surprise about the break-up had abated. The only way forward for me was to work, work, work. All my efforts were focused on the house for a year and a half and I started to feel great—never better, in fact.

One day a friend told me about a competition. It was with the television show *Better Homes and Gardens*, and first prize was $25,000 to spend at Mitre 10. All you had to do was make a short film showing your accomplishments. Since many people told me that it would be impossible for anyone else to win, I thought I'd better enter. Every day after school my boyfriend, Angus and I would film another snippet using a borrowed camera. We put in a lot of inspired effort, edited it and sent it off. The next thing I knew, the producer called and told me the team would come up in a few days time to film a segment as I was one of the finalists. I woke up at 4 am every day, weeding and cleaning to make things look as good as possible.

Winning the competition completely threw me. I spent a whole week afterwards (fortunately it was school holidays) smiling to myself and occasionally letting forth an inane giggle. It was unbelievable. It proved to me that I'd been right after all—I wasn't mad to do what I've done!

Building has been even more fun than I imagined, coupled with some truly hard work. I've proved to myself that I can actually do it, which very likely means you can too. After all, why not?

I wish you well as you embark on your own fantastic adventure, and I hope this book will accompany you on your way.

PLANNING

THE ARBITRARY COUNCIL

DEVELOPMENT APPROVAL

....
Date

....
Authorised Officer

In this section, you'll learn how to turn your ideas into a workable project (I have some interesting new angles for you if you're stuck) and how to make the most of your funds. You'll also find out how to decide whether your relationship can stand the strain of building or renovating. Do you dare to go it alone?

2

Don't be intimidated by the size of a project. I know it can look daunting, but overcome this by breaking it into smaller steps. Do you think you could lay one brick? Just one, single brick, laid straight, true and level? I bet you could if you had enough time and a good spirit level. After the first brick, lay a second. After an invigorating coffee break with some dainty pastries, lay a third... Now keep going. This is how you build a house.

THE OPTIONS

You might already have some seeds germinating in your mind, but how do you begin making your dream a reality? There is much to think about, but careful planning now will make the project run a lot more smoothly later. These are some of the options you may find yourself considering.

Renovating without altering your external structure

If you already have perfectly good spaces or no room to extend or you live in an apartment, then your limits are defined by the outer shell of your existing structure. Your only concern will be to determine which walls are load bearing if you wish to alter the floor plan. You can check this by going up into the roof space. Does anything rest on any of the walls? If so, it is a load-bearing wall and you will need to be very careful about how you proceed. If you are at all uncertain, seek professional help.

Renovations to your existing structure can include general fixing, decorating, and perhaps ripping out the old bathroom or kitchen. Your renovation could be as small as painting the kitchen cupboards or as big as blowing out the whole interior. Most of this you could do yourself, with the exception of any plumbing and wiring. It is illegal (not to mention dangerous) to do electrical work without a licence. Plumbing legalities are similar, but you are allowed to work on plumbing not connected to the town system.

Renovating with partial demolition and extension

This is very common in Australia, as countless old lean-tos are no longer considered desirable by the new owners. When they first appeared, lean-tos were used to house innovations such as indoor laundries and toilets. Little thought appears to have gone into many of these structures, and often natural light has been stolen from back rooms by a narrow lean-to blocking up the rear windows.

Now, the old fibro lean-tos are making way for extensive—and expensive—structures that hopefully work more sympathetically with the main building.

Extending

Your house may be a bit small, perhaps, but there's nothing really wrong with it. If this is your situation, you may decide to attach some rooms to the back, side or top, wherever there's room. The cheapest way is to erect a structure separate from the house, and this can work well if you need room for an office, a studio, a teenage (or parent) retreat, etc. You could attach it to your existing house with a covered walkway. I love the idea of a group of buildings. I don't even mind an old outside laundry as it means you don't have to listen to the washing machine. In my house we often need personal space, so although the house is huge it's still not sufficiently private and could benefit from a garden extension.

A regular ground floor extension to the rear is the most common way to extend your living area. Going up a storey is prohibitively pricey, but if money is no object, it could be another option. However, this is almost impossible to do yourself, as you need to work at lightning speed when the roof is removed! In some cases, it can involve such major surgery that you might be better off rebuilding from the ground up.

Building from scratch

There is something very appealing about being able to incorporate all your ideas into a design of your own. If you are renovating a house in awful condition, it might be cheaper and easier to bulldoze and build anew. But if the house has merit and it's old, do whatever you can to keep it! They don't make them like that any more. An old house will also have settled onto its foundations and into its problems, while a new house is a wild card. If a house has stood for hundred years, it could be good for another hundred, but there is no telling what problems a new one will develop.

THE PRACTICALITIES

While this book looks mainly at the process an owner-builder goes through, much of what I describe is also applicable to the simplest renovation. It's all about planning well and having the confidence to make your dream come to life! You can easily rough out your own plans and it's tremendously exciting to do. I was constantly drawing ideas on the back of napkins and envelopes, and eventually consolidated the ideas over months of delicious deliberating.

When you have sketched out your ideas, take the rough drawing to a draftsman or architect and they will prepare the plans formally and technically for you. They can also provide you with an engineer. Often they will try changing things they think don't work. Listen carefully to them but don't be pressured into doing things their way. Speak to a couple of professionals before committing yourself, as some of them have very clear ideas of how every house in the world should look, including yours. They might try to sell you the architect's services—and fees—for re-designing your building. Work with someone who you think can understand what *you* want. Be strong, you are the one who will ultimately have to build the bloody thing, and you are their boss after all.

Tell your architect or draftsman that you intend to build the house yourself, if you do. Ask for very detailed drawings—you want the dimensions of every bolt included and they must be sure to exclude nothing, no matter how minor.

Though I had specified exactly what I wanted, my architects still tried to change things by just drawing them a different way and not even consulting me. On the other hand, if they had said how expensive the Hi-Span beams that support my second storey would be, I would have changed the plans myself. I was also adamant about wanting wooden floors, but they wrote Structafloor (which is a sheeting you use for laying carpets on) on the plans because that's what's usually requested.

Building a picture

As you plan your house, it helps to ask yourself a series of questions. This will not only help you to determine what's really important to you, but it will also get you inspired. Try these questions to get you started:

◆ Who will be living in the house? Are there going to be any young children, adolescents or elderly? Are the in-laws likely to spend their nineties in your care? Do you want to have paying guests? Are you planning dual occupancy at any time?

◆ What are the needs, present and projected, of these people?

◆ How many bedrooms do you need, and what size should they be?

◆ What's the placement of the bedrooms? Do you want to have children near you or as far away as possible?

◆ Do you want any wardrobes in the bedrooms? Any walk-ins? I have a walk-in for the first time in my life and it's fabulous. It doubles as a dressing room, so I don't have to wake my partner by turning on any lights in the bedroom if I get up earlier than him.

◆ How many bathrooms do you want, and what will they contain: showers, bathtubs, spas, fountains, saunas, plunge pools, gyms, rainforests? When you plan the wet areas, bear in mind the plumbing will be more economical to do if it's all close together.

◆ Do you need access to bathrooms from bedrooms? This is a very newfangled concept. Bathrooms used to be *outside* the house, then they crept in to the back of the house, and now they are right there with us, next to where we sleep. This is good for the elderly perhaps, but so far, I prefer walking a few extra yards.

◆ Do you want a separate toilet? This is a concept that I don't understand, but it is one that is popular in Australia. If you want a separate toilet, install a little hand basin in it so that people don't have to go to another room to wash their hands.

◆ Do you want an open-plan kitchen or a separate one? Historically, the kitchen was never really seen. The current fashion is to let it all hang out open-plan style, which has the advantages of not excluding the cook and providing airflow. It can also look good. However, it isn't always desirable, as you can't close the door on the kitchen with all its possible cooking smells and noise, and it isn't as cosy.

◆ What size kitchen do you need? I initially planned a big one, being married to an accomplished chef who had special requests. My own present needs are more modest, and a tiny kitchen would be enough. I can't say I don't enjoy the extra bench space, though!

◆ What about a pantry? It was one of my dreams alongside the Aga and the rose-snipping secateurs. My grandparents had one. It was really cold as it was vented from the outside and smelled like Festis (a Swedish kid's drink) and all the special occasion food you could wish for. You were only allowed a quick look and then you had to go, as the pantry was a forbidden area for kids. I love stocking my pantry, and to see rows of food in baskets and gleaming glass jars, complete with a reassuring stock of wine on the bottom layers fills me with satisfaction.

◆ Do you want a separate dining room? Dining rooms are fun, but modern society is gradually doing away with them, as dining has become so informal. My parents have one, and it is a large and festive room closed away behind tall bubbly glass doors. As kids, we were always excited if the dining room was going to be used as it meant better food.

◆ Do you want outdoor areas, pergolas, terraces, pools, tennis courts? It's good to plan for them at an early stage so they interact well with the house. Maybe you'll want shelter, cooking facilities, or special lighting. In warm places like Australia we have the potential for gorgeous outside areas and leafy informal party settings. Let your backyard act as a 'room'. Plan for this now.

◆ What sort of storage do you require? I love anything built-in, as it's so practical, but perhaps you prefer the flexibility that moveable storage—

such as wardrobes—can bring. Will you store wine? Do you need an attic, a basement? Think storage now, so you don't have to slap up a tin hold-all afterwards because you forgot to adequately plan your space. I like secret compartments and have included some hidden storage areas. I considered including a historical-style priest's hole or James Bond-like turning fireplace but thought it would be too much work (although fun!).

- What sort of living area/s do you want? Do you want several small ones, and what would their purpose be? Is a large one better than two small ones? I have a tiny television room and a big open all-purpose room. We don't have a word for 'living' room in Swedish—after all, don't you live in all the rooms? Instead, we usually have a 'big' room, or a 'fine' room. The fine room is only used for best or formal occasions and is not a concept I like, but the big room idea works well for me.

- Do you want a separate laundry? You can incorporate it into the kitchen or bathroom, if you wish. Mine, however, is separate and I like it that way as it keeps the smelly sock mountain isolated! I put a laundry chute made from a section of flue in the wall of my son's room: now the socks fall straight into the laundry basket! This only works if you plan the kid's room above the laundry, of course.

- How about a home office? Will any business be conducted from the house? If so, consider the traffic flow through the house. You might prefer the office to be in a separate structure to keep people out of your home, or at the very least placed in the front of the house.

- Do you have room for a garage or a carport? In places like Sydney, you're lucky if you can find a park in the same street as your house. Here around Adelaide, there seems to be a minimum of one garage attached to every single house, with a connecting door into the house so you need not go outdoors at all. Many new houses are fronted by a double garage that dominates the streetscape. I have never felt much of an urge for a garage but I do have a carport. You can get more money for a house with a garage, as the people who can pay more have expensive

cars that need sheltering. A garage can also provide useful storage, and if you have boats and motorbikes and other bits you'll have somewhere to put them.

- How do you arrange vehicle access from the road, assuming you can?

- Do you dream of palm-filled conservatories, lofty studios, soundproof music rooms, smelly ferret playrooms? Whatever takes your fancy can be in your house. I hankered after a large quail garden enclosure attached to the house, for the sake of the cute little eggs, fried on toast, and the belief that quails ate a certain local pest insect, but then I thought of the snakes a bird enclosure would attract and changed my mind. I also no longer like to keep birds enclosed. No matter how strange your desire, write it down at this stage. You can always delete it later. This is dream time.

- Would you like a home cinema, a library, a workshop? If it's important, add it to your plan.

- How will you control the temperature? Are you planning any solid brick chimney fireplaces or do plain flues suffice? A solid brick chimney could be the hardest thing of all to build. If the house falls down, the chimney must be strong enough to still remain standing. I don't have the skill myself, and I find flues satisfactory, although I do think brick chimneys look nicer.

- If you want a rainwater tank, where you will place it?

- How will you position the house? North–south is ideal in Australia, as you should aim to capture the northern light as much as possible. However, if you have a block on a street facing another direction, there may be little you can do about it. In Sweden, a country of little light most of the year, the houses of whole streets are sometimes angled to catch whatever light is available. Take the time to chart your block for movement of light, and then carefully consider which rooms you want to receive morning or afternoon sun. In Australia, avoid large windows that will cop the boiling afternoon sun in the west.

◆ Are passive energy and sustainability of concern to you? If they aren't yet, think about them now. You can improve the energy consumption of your house immensely with some simple design principles. For instance, since the Second World War, many buildings in Australia have been built in brick veneer. This style was created due to shortages in material, as builders needed to stretch out supplies. However, it offers little in thermal value. If you wanted to make a brick veneer house thermally efficient, you would reverse everything and have the bricks on the *inside*, and the cladding on the *outside*. But most people won't do that, as it would look cheap. As people become more aware of these things and energy costs escalate, passive energy principles will be a winner. As with all new ideas, we just have to wait a while for general acceptance. Houses that are cheap to build are sometimes expensive to run. Through good design you can limit your energy consumption. For more money upfront you can collect, heat and recycle your own water, and even generate your own energy. I collect all our water, heat it through a combined solar and wood-fired system and recycle it in the paddock. I also solar heat the pool water, though it is run by an electric pump that isn't solar powered, much to my regret. Had I been able to afford it, I would have installed a small wind-powered unit on my roof, as it is often windy here.

> **One small way to reduce electricity consumption is to ensure the air flows readily behind the fridge. If the fridge is on a wooden floor, you can cut holes to enable cool air to enter behind it. Energy-saving ideas can be as simple as that.**

◆ Do you have views? How can you best incorporate them? Large windows are not necessarily better—think of a tiny aperture in a Greek islands home framing the blue Aegean with whitewashed walls. My best views are to the south and passive energy design prohibits large windows in that direction. As a result, the windows are not enormous but there is no need. The views are still there, just smaller. The fashion of inserting big glass windows and sliding doors, even where the view is that of the

neighbour's fence, has come about because the labour costs in the actual building of the walls is more expensive than the cost of glass for windows and doors. Don't automatically lean towards this trend. If you are doing the work yourself, the wall may now be cheaper than the window. Carefully consider your design. Climatically, lots of glass could be unwise and you might need to consider double and triple glazing, which will really elevate the cost.

◆ What ceiling height do you want? High ceilings are nice, airy and cool; low ones can be cosy, warm and much cheaper! Measure the ceilings and other dimensions in an existing room that you like. Think of your climate, too. You'll have to pay for the ongoing heating and cooling.

◆ Will your house have one storey or more? The site will help to determine this. I wanted the feeling of space that a central void in my house would give so I drew two storeys and left the middle bit out. The result is beautifully airy and open. I also like incredibly tiny and cosy buildings, but this house isn't one of those. My next home could well be a one-roomed miner's cottage you have to duck to get into.

I'm sure you can add to this list of questions. The answers will kick-start the design process. For instance, you might decide that you want a U-shaped two-bedroom house for noise reduction and privacy, one bathroom, a kitchenette with laundry included, a large separate enclosed garden building for giving folkdance lessons, with a shaded cat-proof courtyard in between. Since the variations on this theme are endless, I can't understand why most houses look pretty much the same. It's often only at the wealthy end of the market that houses show the benefit of interesting choices, but it doesn't have to be that way. With a little ingenuity, everyone can make his or her house unique.

Dream at this stage and put in everything you want. Then make another list, one that states the bare minimum. These lists could differ a lot. Every item you add equates to more money and time that you have to find. Is it worth it to you? Evaluate everything critically. Play with pen and paper. Move rooms around, look at how air and sound will move through the house, see

what's practical. This is one of the most pleasurable things you can do—you're building without getting dirty and, so far, it's free! In order to get an idea of room sizes, measure the room you're in and then compare it to the ones on your wish list. I only wanted rooms that were generously sized, so that's what I built.

When you have a fair idea of what your dream home might look like, make a cardboard model so you're really able to 'walk around' it. I spotted many design faults in my house after doing so. If you have buckets of Lego you can use that.

A building can only be regarded as successful if it performs well. Looks aren't everything. Is the traffic flow poorly managed? Are the kids' bedrooms directly on top of yours or vice versa? Can the house be easily maintained; is it possible to reach the second-floor windows or do you need a cherry picker for cleaning them? Consider likely daily scenarios such as unloading groceries. Why not put the kitchen at the front of the house, instead of the bedrooms? Don't do anything just because that's the way it's always been done. Question why.

THE NICETIES

What will your house look like? There are endless ways of putting exactly the same material together to create very different outcomes. It's your personal style that will make the difference. Give me the material allotted to the construction of any ordinary house and I will design it my way. It doesn't have to cost more to create an attractive and interesting house instead of a low-profile box, but it requires more effort. This is where you come in. As Lord Leighton said in 1888 in a presidential address to the National Association for the Advancement of Art and its Application to Industry:

Is it not a wholesome sense dawning among us that even a private dwelling should not offend, nay, should conciliate the eye of the passer-by in our public thoroughfares? ...I acknowledge with joy that there is...

At present, we see many houses being built featuring identical showy fake fronts. As a result, there is a growing anti mass-production movement amongst owner-builders; they are revolting against this blandness. Personally I like things that look as if actual humans have made them, and made them with real thought. Good architecture can bring happiness, and you don't need a lot of money to have style!

I believe your environment helps to form you as much as you help to form it. This is your chance to have input into something as big as a house. Hopefully it will stand a long time and act as a source of inspiration to others. It is extraordinarily easy to be different. If that is what you want, of course! Most people want the approval of their peers and if you express personal ideas you may not be as easily accepted. Some people end up putting aside their own attitudes and beliefs, accepting those of others instead in order to belong. They may not even be aware of what they're doing. But the arts evolve and progress because of people who refuse to accept the rules of fashion, so follow your instincts and don't be afraid to stand out from the crowd.

Naturally, if you are doing this in order to acquire an inoffensive investment property, it might be best to listen to the real estate agent who says, 'I think beige and brown speckled carpet is safe and nice, and cream-painted walls will match the exterior cream brick façade.' If, however, you are doing it for yourself, search your heart for answers. Do you remember something from your childhood that makes you happy for no real reason? I do, I have a very clear image of a rippled piece of glass above a door in the room where we used to sleep at my grandparents. Seeing that type of glass now makes me feel happy, safe and tucked into bed. For an added feel-good factor, incorporate your memories into your ideas.

What is your background? Look to that for inspiration. Whatever your heritage, whether you're from good convict stock or a recent arrival, your bones will be steeped in an architectural tradition that makes you feel good. See what was built historically, anywhere! There is so much more available for you to use as inspiration for your home than the all-too-boring

standard. Remember, at this point you haven't committed to anything, and you can swing from Alpine hut to Jamaican cabin without any money leaving your wallet.

Out of place, says who?

I find the current trend of impersonal dwelling designs quite depressing. Look at old buildings from various periods all over the world. Many give the impression that they were built to please or amuse. They are full of unnecessary space, unexpected curly bits and crenellations, gargoyles, surprising painted spots and wooden cut-outs. While many of these amazing buildings are the result of a gross imbalance of power and income, many are cheap peasant buildings where an attempt to be attractive on a shoestring budget was the motivating principle. What has happened to us all in the last 70 or so years? The human mind needs visual surprises if it is to stay alert. Don't let your mind slacken off and become dull!

A word of caution: you can have too much of a good thing. Pulling too many styles together in an ad-hoc way can appear chaotic, but with care you should be able to weld ideas together into a successful style that is perhaps uniquely yours. I call my house a combination of Greek island, Australian and Swedish. I designed it to be plain enough so it wouldn't be too hard to build. What isn't there is as important as what is.

In today's world, we are more willing to accept surprises in a building if it is explained with a technological or practical reasoning. Strange constructions that are unmotivated by anything stronger than 'I felt like it' will have a hard time getting accepted. For instance, a building with a sloping wall aimed at the sun, covered in adjustable-angle solar panels will not be questioned, but a building shaped like a concrete ox lying on its side will certainly provide plenty of controversy unless you can justify it with a practical explanation.

There is so much charm and beauty in the world, but how can you go about bringing some into your home? Perhaps the only way is to discard all the

standard ideas and make the house a blank canvas. Re-think why you are putting things where. Is it coming from you heart, or is it social and environmental conditioning? Would you do the house the same if you were living in Milwaukee or Kyoto? Balance your practical concerns with your aesthetic needs. For example, altering your roof profile from the 'norm' is one way to give your house a little extra style, but it could raise the cost of construction. The steeper the pitch, the greater the cost. Where snowfalls are likely, a steep roof serves a practical purpose as it makes it easier for the snow to slide off. On the other hand, if you want a near-flat roof you should be aware that it could prove unsuitable in areas of high rainfall. I wanted a Greek-style totally flat roof section to use as an elevated outdoor area but had to change my plans as the roof would have been too hard to seal, according to the architects.

We all want a place that we can call our own, and that feeling of ownership is often more important than any aesthetic quality it may have. But, while we can avoid reading a book by not opening it, we can't ignore the buildings that fill our streets. When you draw your house, think of it as a work of art that will be looked at by people every day. Scratch your aesthetic itch. Infuse a touch of joy into your design.

THE RESPONSIBILITIES

It is only in very recent times that we have bothered to employ builders to do the work for us. Throughout history we plebs have always done the building ourselves. The standard may not have been very consistent, but no one was there to inspect our potentially sloppy thatch. One of the reasons there are so many ruins scattered in the Australian countryside is because of inferior building material. Without lime and cement to make mortar with, the stones have come loose. Without modern methods of pest control the termites have crunched merrily through the timbers, causing them to collapse. These failings were not the original owner-builder's fault—Australia was a hard place to build in for the settlers. When you abandon a building in Australia, it's only a matter of time before nature takes over.

Things are different today. Materials are often far superior and techniques have also improved. Quality is now mainly dependent on the builder. In my experience, owner-builders will rarely cheat as this is truly *their* building, *their future home* and they care about it passionately. Of course, it's possible that they may make mistakes through lack of knowledge. Paid contractors are far more likely to produce substandard work because they couldn't be bothered to do a good job, even though they have the skills. However, as an owner-builder, you will still need to comply with all the necessary legislation and regulations.

Building regulations

There are two different approvals you can apply for: planning permission and building approval. You may need to get both before you can start on your project so talk to your council about what they require. The building code differs from area to area. It is an intensely complex set of documents, regularly updated, and little is left to chance. Remember that it is done for your benefit no matter how obstructive it can seem at times. For example, depending on the prevailing wind strength in your region, your building will need a certain level of wind resistance. Obviously, a house in a cyclone-prone area needs to be stronger than one that isn't, but I can't see any reason why you couldn't go overboard in strength wherever you live. Roofs do blow off all over the place, even the ones designed and constructed according to the rules.

For fire reasons you weren't allowed to build wooden houses in the cities after the mid-nineteenth century. Too many all-engulfing fires had consumed too much property. In fact, many building regulations exist to prevent your property from burning. Others are to prevent the roof from collapsing or people from falling down stairs. In order to ensure that you comply, your council will come to inspect your handy work usually at certain specified stages, eg. prior to pouring the slab, prior to putting on the roof, and prior to lining the wet area walls. My council inspector used to pop over quite often initially, perhaps out of curiosity to see what I could do. When he inspected the first roof section he said that he'd never

doubted that I could do it, and I stopped having these impromptu visits. It used to be nerve-racking not knowing when I would have authority descend on me to check whether I was doing the right thing. Was I working to the accepted standard?

There are a few laws these days that apply to owner-builders. They vary according to state or territory so check with your local Building Services Authority. As a rough guide, you need no permit if the work will cost less than around $5000 (unless your house is of historical interest, in which case you can't do much without advice). For work costing between $5000 and $11,000 you'll need an owner-builder's permit, which just requires you to fill in some forms. If your projected costs will exceed $11,000 you might in some areas need an owner-builder's licence, which requires you to take a short course. This is all good and fine if it helps you to acquire useful skills but don't be put off by the technicalities or potential requirements. I didn't need a course where I lived.

The council will also put a time restriction on your work. You will have 12 months to substantially commence the project, which basically means to lay down foundations, and three years in which to complete it. They will usually grant you an extension for 12 months but no more. You can understand why time limits are controlled this way. Would you want to live next door to a potentially rat-infested ugly construction site indefinitely? By keeping your site tidy, you will avoid any unnecessary attention from the authorities.

You may also have Work Cover obligations. Again, check the laws for your state or territory.

As an owner-builder, you are only allowed to build one house every five years. This should be plenty—some people can take ten years to finish their project! The ruling is in order to stop you from pretending to be an owner-builder when you are really a professional builder. The reason some try to slip by as owner-builders is to avoid mandatory insurance. If you are that keen and fast, do yourself a favour and take the proper builder's licence course.

Public liability

Yes, unfortunately you will be held liable in the event of an accident. This is *your* site and you are responsible for what occurs on it. Insurance is not compulsory, unless you use a finance organization that requires it, but ask yourself whether you could afford it if a worker, hardware delivery person, charity collector or someone else claimed negligence on your site? I don't think so. You would probably face financial ruin of such severity that you would never recover unless you won the lottery. Sadly, owner-builders have a wealth of stories about being refused insurance. Professional builders work for a short time on each house and use a special construction insurance, which is very expensive. To have the same kind of insurance extended over many years would be ludicrously expensive. In addition, you cannot get a 'house' insured until it is 'finished'. My situation was as follows: I had completely finished one section and was living in it, was commencing building on the other bit and wanted to insure the finished, independent section as a 'house' being extended. Technically, it was! Eventually, it was proving so hard to get any kind of insurance that I gave up and had no insurance whatsoever until I had a roof up and could insure the whole thing as a 'house', not a 'site'. However, insurance does give peace of mind and is recommended, if you can find a suitable one.

What about insuring yourself? You might like to consider a policy covering your own person. If something happens to you, you can pay someone else to finish the job. Again, I thought I would take responsibility for myself and not get any.

Safety laws

People get injured and even die at work all the time. In an effort to halt this, humans created Occupational Health and Safety laws. This is a brilliant set of documents, making workplaces around the nation safer and better. It includes tough laws complete with penalties for the law-breakers. Do the OHS laws apply to the owner-builder? That depends! The regulations *do not apply to premises only occupied as a private dwelling*. However, if you

employ someone you become an employer and suddenly you are subject to all the employer provisions of the Act. So if you are working by yourself on your residential house, they don't apply. But you should still observe good standards of safety, just for your own sake!

If your work will exceed $250,000 or include any demolition or asbestos removal, no matter how low the estimated cost, you legally need an Occupational Health and Safety plan. This is a paper that includes details of arrangements for managing OHS incidents, site safety rules and details for ensuring all persons on the site are informed of the rules as well as safe work method statements for all activities that are risky. You may think it's unnecessary but it is required by law. You can download the entire OHS Act from the Internet, and pick out the bits relevant to you.

You should also contact Work Cover in your state and ask for a Sub-contractor Pack. Under Clause 229 in the OHS regulations, a subcontractor *must not commence work* unless they have been provided with a copy of your management plan if the law requires you to have one (see above). You don't want subbies on your doorstep ready to work that you have to let go because of insufficient paperwork. The subbies probably won't care but it is in your own best interests to comply with the legislation in order to prevent trouble at a later date. Remember, pleading ignorance will not be considered a valid excuse in court.

So, did I adhere to the safety rules? No, sadly, the thought didn't occur to me. I thought I was responsible only for myself until a subcontractor told me I was using some unsafe practices that I had to stop. Oops! I think I also sometimes took a perverse pride in being able to do something in as dangerous a fashion as possible. Perhaps I was scared of being called a girlie wuss otherwise.

Be aware that you can be fined up to $200,000 for non-compliance with workplace safety. It is a potentially serious issue and you need to consider how much it could really cost you. The building industry is full of gory stories about people having accidents. Every year people die. Think about it. It's too late to change your mind about safety then.

While some of the accidents are plain unfortunate, many are preventable. For example, a lot of accidents happen because of poor housekeeping. Housekeeping basically means tidiness so don't leave stuff lying around for people to trip over. Imagine walking backwards with a large sheet of glass ready to install and tripping over a small obstacle on the ground.

Take the necessary precautions and look out for yourself and others. If anything ever happens on your site, even to yourself, you want to be able to prove in court that you had done the right thing.

3

MONEY

—'doing the laundering was never so easy!'

THE AMAZING NEW
ACME
MONEY MAKER!!!

In which we find somewhere we hadn't previously looked and learn how to borrow as little as possible

Obtainable at all leading hardware and department stores

Mortgage is French for 'death pledge'—that should tell you something! 'Why Struggle When You Can Borrow?' 'Pay Back Your Home Loan Sooner!' 'Home Loans to Suit You!' 'Borrow from the Good Guys!' The lending industry is bigger than the Big Pineapple; it encourages you to buy house and land packages and to borrow as much as possible. The lenders *want* you to owe. It is what pays their wages. They don't want you living for free in a felted yurt on a remote coastal block managing a commercial deer herd when they could have you making regular payments for 25 years on a suburban brick box. Who cares if you die in the effort to pay the mortgage? They certainly don't.

MINIMIZING THE MORTGAGE

We once borrowed 95 per cent of the value of an investment unit, with barely sufficient income to cover the necessary expenses. The mobile lending person sitting cosily at our kitchen table didn't care. He wondered if we didn't want to borrow some more money while we were at it, as it would come in really handy later when we started building on our land. The mortgage industry is one with potential for unscrupulous methods: it wants you to borrow lots of money and it wants you to borrow it immediately. It's great to have the option to borrow, but you should work out how much you'll be paying in interest. Don't overcommit yourself, as the banks won't think twice about repossessing if you can't meet repayments because of rising interest rates or a temporary loss of income, for instance. Will a two-month illness be detrimental to your finances? Then perhaps you should insure your income. Otherwise, make sure you always have enough cash put aside to cover a couple of repayments in case of economic disaster.

In order to reduce your borrowing needs see if your family wants to invest with you. It won't hurt to ask! Perhaps they have paid off their own debt, and could extend themselves financially. Some friends of mine built a granny flat in their garden for their ageing father, and in exchange for their care of him, he was able to help them buy the kind of house they could not have contemplated otherwise. Think laterally.

Do-it-yourselvers can find it hard to borrow for their constructions, but the banks will readily lend money for the land. So, you could borrow as much as possible for the land and keep any cash towards building. However, if finances are tight, it will not be possible for you to bring the mortgage down at the same time as trying to save towards building. I couldn't have done it the way I did unless I had renovated a house first and sold it for a profit, which freed up enough capital to buy land outright. That was three years' work that paid off well. Perhaps that's an option you could consider, instead of aiming for your dream house straight away.

If you have borrowed money to purchase land, you might choose to live in a temporary dwelling while money builds up again. Or you may decide to live

through a renovation. This temporary accommodation can be made as homely as you like, but just ensure that it's legal or the council can fine you for squatting (see the chapter on 'Moving in early').

If you are selling a house to finance a new home, you are in a great position as you are already in the property market and will hopefully have benefited from rising property values. If you are selling a home in the city and moving to the country you're in an even better position.

Many people want everything *now*, even if there is no cash available. Why wait when you can borrow? My advice is to buy the best house you can, or the best land you can afford, then wait until you've earned some more money instead of borrowing extra for the renovations. You will save a fortune in staggering interest costs and although it means the work proceeds more slowly, it will give you time to think carefully about things before you steam ahead.

Town or country

Most people have to go to work, and this will obviously dictate where they can live. However, I think most major cities are impossibly priced for what they offer. You can end up mortgaged for a couple of generations in order to be allowed to live in a distant suburb. How do ordinary first-home buyers find the money to buy anything in the cities? Life is so short, barely long enough to pay back the debt. If you have to work every minute of the day just to stay afloat financially, surely something is wrong?

One way to escape the burden of enormous debt is to move to the country. If you don't care about where you live or don't need to be close to a major town you can get your hands on extremely good value rural land. There are a few issues you need to consider carefully though, before making any decision to move. When my husband and I decided to try the rural life, we worried about where our income would come from. Would there be any jobs around? The options were not the same as in the city, and I commuted for three hours a day for a year before I was able to start working locally. Salaries may be lower in the country, too. Would you settle for a reduced income in exchange for cheaper property?

Initially, I also worried a little about never again being able to buy into a city, as the property values in the country wouldn't rise accordingly. But, deciding to live in the country is a lifestyle choice too. I now live in a beautiful and culturally rich area, which is just over an hour by car to town or 15 minutes to work (without any traffic lights), for the price of a one-bedroom apartment in a very average suburb in Sydney. Rural living offers many benefits that towns don't have. There's a more friendly and relaxed outlook, virtually no crime or pollution, and a greater sense of community. When we first moved here, it took less than 24 hours before the newsagent knew me by name.

Some aspects of country life may not be quite what you imagine. When my husband and I planned our move, I pictured myself wearing jodhpurs and tweeds, gathering kindling in a refined way as I wandered through misty woodlands. Unaware of what land ownership entails, we innocently planned to become primary producers and claim enormous tax deductions to offset our 'real' jobs. I wanted a pretty location in order to run a bed and breakfast, on a major tourist route so I could have a weekend gallery as well. Perfect!

In reality, owning land means the maintenance of fences, otherwise livestock will break out or in and eat your plants. My paddocks have one main purpose, and that is to keep me at a distance from my neighbours. I know now that I will never become a successful producer of crustaceans, miniature cattle, quail, or wattle seed. I am certainly no farmer. Owning land also means that I am constantly waging war on weeds. I am the proud owner of a selection of the most noxious weed species. I have to use a brushcutter to hack at horribly healthy and prickly weeds that lash out at my car as I drive past. If I don't keep them under control, they grow woody and scrape long scratches in the duco as I try to run them down.

Of course, you could avoid this by buying a bush block, which won't require much care as it is an established ecosystem already. However, this has the drawback of you possibly not being allowed to clear any of it, and comes with the annual threat of bushfire.

Part of my land is planted with natives, where little bright-green finches weave in and out of my stand of spiky cat-repellent trees and fat sleepy

lizards bask on the paths. Wattle season brings a harvest of sneezes as it turns the bottom paddock sweet scented and bright yellow. Another section is open for grazing, where my friendly goat Poddy shares the space with two visiting horses. Soaring crowds of yellow-crested cockatoos decimate my almond crop and one area is filled with assorted fruit trees, remarkably prolific for their lack of care. There is a kitchen garden for herbs and vegies, and I have filled garden beds with lavender, rosemary, roses and other things that don't need much water.

I love it all and, if you think you can survive without the big city luxuries (wider choice of entertainment, more education opportunities, greater choice of employment), I don't think you can go wrong trying out country living. It's also good to keep in mind that, in the future, more people may be able to work from home and then location won't be so critical. My advice is to invest in beautiful property out of the cities now, while there's still good value to be had! There are lots of glorious old stone buildings in need of repair. The countryside is scattered with cottages, churches and Freemason's halls just waiting for you to come and play house.

Two's company

Relocating is not the only option for reducing your financial outlay, however. You might be able to change a place into dual occupancy, as the cities keep cramming in more people. That way you will halve your costs. Take an ordinary house and convert it into an upstairs/downstairs area, or two units side by side.

Proportionately, larger places can offer better value. The old hippie commune idea may not be your thing but it can be worthwhile to consider several friends pooling together to buy a bigger place and then changing it into individual smaller residences. Some people I know bought a grand seafront Victorian and converted it into four apartments. Some things can be shared, like a really decent laundry or a tool shed with everything owned by the group. Do five people really need five drills, five lawnmowers or five vacuum cleaners? All that added storage just detracts from the available space.

Another way to generate income is to have boarders. If you are a single parent, it could be really nice to share with a person in the same situation. You can share care of the kids, you don't have to cook every day if you take turns, and your kids will benefit hugely from this extended situation, as there are more kids to play and bicker with. The price you pay is the need to tolerate constant noise—but if you have more than one offspring you will already lead a noisy life. I would have considered this if my situation had been different. As it was, Angus was ten when my marriage broke up, and so didn't need the extra care, and the house was in no fit state to take on extra kids. Had I been a single parent when he was much smaller, I would perhaps have lived in a larger house so we could retain our privacy as well as reap the benefits of sharing. Parents of young kids need lots of support and people around them. I'm sure some women stay in unsupportive relationships with their partners for fear of being alone, and poor. Perhaps they could consider merging with someone they are not in a relationship with, for company and funds.

GETTING THE MOST FOR YOUR MONEY

Saving money just means not spending it. Making the money you have go that little bit further requires a bit more ingenuity!

Discounts

You will need to buy things for your renovation or building project, but how can you get the stuff you need for less? Look for discounts here and there; after all, a penny saved is a penny earned!

The same goods can vary a lot in price. Check out the competition. Tell the supplier how much you want to pay. You never know how much you can save!

If you're lucky, your hardware shop will give you a builder's discount, even if you don't have a builder's licence. My hardware would sometimes beat the prices down even further, without me having to ask. Find the store you want to shop in, speak to the manager about what you are planning to do and ask what sort of discount they will give you. You will be spending a

fortune before you're done, so it is in their best interests to keep you as a customer. My first Christmas as a pretend builder I gave the hardware shop a carton of beer, saying, 'This is for discounts and for never patronizing me.'

Ask other shops for cash discounts. They may comply, but you'll never know unless you ask.

When you see an advertisement saying 'Store closing—up to 40% discount', go shopping for tiles, plumbing or whatever they're selling. Even if completing the bathroom is a long way down your list, you know what you'll need for it and things can be stored in the meantime. I bought a pallet of great value second-hand red brick pavers before I even had a plan for what I wanted paved. When opportunity knocks, open the wallet. I only bought one thing I didn't need—a ceramic drain thingy.

Factory scratched and dented

There are shops specializing in scratched or dented merchandise where you can make huge savings. Do you *truly* care if the cook top has a tiny scratch? Chances are the scratch is on the back, anyway. Your Auntie Emma was possibly going to scratch it for you the first time she visited, so you might as well buy it scratched from the start and get a discount.

Sometimes there are auctions dedicated to 'Scratch and Dent', but do your homework before you bid. If you know exactly what you are looking for you will know how much it costs in the shop and can bid accordingly. I got a perfect Smeg stove for nearly half price! As soon as I got it home, I put a small dent in the lid myself. Perhaps I could work for the factory that scratches and dents…

Antique shops

You won't save much here, though I have picked up a few bargains over time. Antique shops are usually great for a more expensive highlight. I was for a long time considering what to use for a centrepiece in my terracotta floor in the main area. I had cut a large four-pointed star into the tiles, but it

needed something special recessed in the centre. For six months we tripped over the hole in the floor, before the answer was found in an antique shop: a black cast-iron plaque saying 'Wheatley—Maker—Kapunda'. It's perfect.

Another excellent find was the long polished oar that acts as a towel rail in my bathroom. I set the supporting bolts right into the wall when I laid it. It adds a nice touch.

Recycled and free

I love salvage yards! It is thrilling to go scavenging. The hardest part is keeping the wallet shut. The yards come in a range of price and presentation, as different as your average op shop and a big department store.

One of my very favourite shops has room to move, is light with plenty of air, looks and smells clean and fresh, and you can find what you are looking for as everything is sorted and in immaculate order. Most stuff is in great condition and of high quality. It's so tidy you can go in there dressed for town and not be ruffled when you leave. They also stock all sorts of antique reproduction locks and handles, and have friendly, helpful staff. Their prices are pretty reasonable, too. There are no dusty bargains lurking in cobwebbed corners, however. These people know the value of their goods.

My other favourite store is one I have to dress especially for. Boots and long jeans are required for snake protection, and possibly heavy-duty gloves for rummaging as well. Only a small portion of the stock is kept indoors; most is stored under rattling corrugated iron sails or out in the open in great jumbled piles. A couple of grumpy old men and a dog I wouldn't want to meet without its owners present run the joint. You will get dirty scavenging but you can unearth some goodies if your eyes are wide open.

If you are considering building with stone, with a bit of luck you can buy an entire house due for demolition very cheaply. Once the easily resaleable things have been removed—like doors, windows and other woodwork—and the roof is gone, the machinery moves in and dumps the wall material on trucks. It then often simply gets thrown out for fill. The manual labour

involved in cleaning and sorting makes this kind of material quite expensive if you buy it through the salvage yard, which is why they may not even bother with it. This is where you come in.

A few years ago, I was out with a friend walking the dog. We came to an absolutely enormous hole in the ground, the shape of an eggcup. It was near a vineyard on the valley floor, and it would have been used for protection against the floods that used to be a regular problem in the area. No longer needed, the hole was being gradually filled in with stone and rubble from old house demolitions. I just wanted to stop all that lovely stone being buried forever! I spoke to the demolishers, and they said they had a house coming up that I could have for the cost of the truck's time in delivering the tonnes of rubble and stone to my place. I very nearly did it, but my husband thought it was a bad idea. A lot of the rubble would have been unusable, and I would have had to sort through everything and cart away the debris. This is only really a budget idea if the house being demolished is near you (or the transport costs will rise too much), and you have the time and energy to do all the necessary sorting.

Some building rubble is very much worth the effort though, so keep your eyes open. I once drove past the local high school when they were in the middle of demolishing an old transportable classroom. There was a big pile of timber lying to the side, all unsorted and with big nails sticking out everywhere. I pulled over and had a chat to the lads pulling it apart, and ended up buying the whole lot for a few hundred dollars. From it, I got a whole lot of fascias, Oregon and old pine that I made furniture from to sell. Plenty of bookshelves have also come from that mixed pile, now milked dry unfortunately.

Our local pub was tearing down their old balcony. My husband had a chat with the blokes and got a pile of 100-year-old jarrah floorboards for free. They form my outdoor table these days.

You can find free things around. Take a peek at skips, for instance. People are no longer permitted to go through rubbish dumps, more is the pity; however, some dumps have a re-sale outlet of salvage items.

Garage sales, auctions, flea markets, car boot sales and classifieds

When I first came to Australia I thought a garage sale involved selling the garage, but I've since discovered this is another great source for bargains. I bought six tall louvre doors for my entry wardrobes for a ridiculously low $5, plenty of broken clear glass for leadlight, two bathroom windows for $30, tools, and a random assortment of timber amongst other finds. I will possibly have a garage sale myself where I'll sell the excess stuff I no longer need.

Finding used stuff is great for people who are looking for adding character or matching their extension with an older house; or people like me, with little money to spare and desiring an older, more worn look. If you buy the doors and windows before you start, you can design the house around them. There are plenty of items to be found—staircases, whole truss structures, bathtubs, flooring, etc.

It's good if you have somewhere to store everything. We didn't and our apartment had windows and things stacked everywhere. I didn't care though; I just wanted to get ready to start building.

The newspapers are another good source. There's usually a whole section devoted to second-hand and leftover building material.

Fixing, mixing and matching your finds

When you get your bargains home, you need to clean them up. When it comes to paint stripping, I find a heat gun is the answer. No messy chemicals are required, and you can sweep up the hard paint flakes when you have finished. You will need a few different widths and shapes of scrapers (there is a nice bent variety for mouldings). Just be very careful not to overheat glass, as it will go 'Ping!' and leave you feeling very foolish as it breaks. Oops! You'll only do that once, I hope.

However, there is a much easier way to strip paint, and that is to drive the whole job to a furniture dipper. They will submerge your crusty old door in a huge vat of acid, and a totally clean version will emerge. You won't recognize

it. The only time I did that was with an old front door that was so nice I thought it deserved a professional treatment. The problem was, however, that all the glue in the door dissolved in the acid and I had to take it apart and reassemble it again. That took so long I might as well have stripped the door by hand.

You really do need to have all your doors and windows before you begin anything, as you will be too busy with other stuff to look for a missing window halfway through the project. Doors will all be slightly different in size, and you'll need to get individual doorframes made.

I passed up on a sash window at a charity auction even though it only sold for $2 because I thought I had to *stop* collecting any more windows. You might have to look at plenty of windows to find ones that are sufficiently similar so as not to make the walls look odd, if that worries you. I decided on mostly sash windows, as they are the easiest to find in my area. I bought any size I could find and matched them afterwards. Unless your house has a flat front requiring windows that all match for a Georgian look, it might not matter much if you mix up the sizes. I have three new windows in this house, 30 or so fixed ones that I've made (I am unable to make windows that actually open and shut), and ten old sashes. The three new ones are Velux openable roof windows, I couldn't get those second hand and together they cost over $3000. Very different from $30!

4

BUILDING AND RENOVATING WITH A PARTNER

IN WHICH WE ARE SHOWN HOW TO KEEP, LOSE, GET, OR OTHERWISE CHANGE OUR RELATIONSHIPS

Before I started building, I was in a long-term relationship. I still am, but with someone else! While I don't think the building project was the only reason my marriage broke up, it was definitely a part of it. Are you in a meaningful partnership with someone? Is the building going to be a joint project? I simply *must* caution you here: many people break up as a result of being an owner-builder couple, no matter how committed they were prior to commencement. The stresses are simply too great for their relationship to withstand.

If your relationship ends, you could lose a lot of money if a practically worthless half-built house is put on the market as the result of the break-up. With the new Australian law of having to wait six years before you sell your finished owner-built house (unless you take out special warranty insurance to cover this contingency) you could be in real trouble. There is little hope of easily recouping your outlay.

Good things can happen though! Life is amazing and offers many surprises. Some couples love building or renovating together. They are able to work as a team, share similar ideas about how things should look, and go on to renovate or build more as they grow in their united strength. It is a great thing if you can do it!

BEFORE YOU BEGIN

To see whether you're suited as a couple to build together, I recommend you do something that will test you both. Tackle a challenging activity that stretches you, forces any issues with discomfort, and shows how well you can work as a team. I suggest roofing and guttering but that's hard to arrange when you have no house to roof yet. Perhaps you could do a really long and uncomfortable hike up a few mountains, carrying your tent and food in rough weather. Think of something hard and unpleasant to do where you will be forced to rely on each other. Experience triumphant highs and crippling lows! Perhaps one of you is more resilient to hardship and will carry the mental load better? Consider whether you would start a business with each other. If you wouldn't, don't consider building together. It's a very similar situation. Remember that it's one thing to share a normal relationship and quite another to place that relationship on a building site.

Building is no picnic and you need to be prepared for your relationship to become strained as things get difficult and your finances are milked dry. Work out some issues prior to commencing. This might seem crass, but if you have talked about potential problems before you even lodge plans with the council you are better prepared. People change too, as they might not initially have realized the enormity of the commitment. Are your energy

levels the same? Do you both think the ideal thing to do on a Thursday night is three hours of stacking bricks after work? Will you resent it if you are the only one doing that? Will you resent it if your partner spends too much time away from the site, pursuing his regular leisure activities?

The following are some purely practical questions you might like to ask each other before you begin.

◆ Who is responsible for what area?

◆ How many hours each week will be devoted to the actual task of building?

◆ Who will do the housework?

◆ Who will do the cooking?

◆ Who will take care of any animals?

◆ How much money and time will be set aside for leisure activities?

◆ Who will control the finances?

◆ If you have children, who will help with homework, drive the kids to tennis, etc?

◆ What happens if you become pregnant?

So many opportunities for argument and resentment arise when you're building together. Take a look at this little scene for example:

> You are busily digging trenches outside, happy in the knowledge that the inside of the house is being cared for. When you finally decide to come in—dirty, hungry, and weak with exhaustion—you find dinner bubbling on the stove. Your children are just coming out of the bath, their beds are warm, clean and inviting, their homework is completed. Happily you have a shower followed by dinner and a drinkie, rejuvenated for another day.

Now imagine this scenario instead:

> You are busily digging trenches outside, happy in the knowledge that inside dinner is cooking, the children are clean with their homework completed, etc. But, when you finally come in, what do you find? Your spouse is sitting down with the paper or in front of the television, perhaps even having a little snooze. There's *no* completed homework, *no* dinner, and *no* clean children. You are totally exhausted and wouldn't have stayed out for so long if you'd thought nothing had been done. Now you have to do everything yourself.

What you are looking at here is a potentially serious source of resentment, perhaps for both of you, as he might have thought you were out there for far too long.

These sorts of issues simply must be agreed upon upfront, so that you don't get any unpleasant surprises later on. I don't mind doing the building work by myself, but I certainly want the laundry folded in exchange! Write things down. Speak up. If you can't agree on things now, you won't be able to agree later. And by then it might be too late…

ADVICE: GIVING AND ACCEPTING IT

As time goes on you will both develop different abilities and preferences for things. If your partner tells you how to do something better or more efficiently, hopefully it's because he possesses a skill you don't yet have, and you are about to learn a better way. But, if *you* tell *him* how to do something and he won't take heed, that's bad. Being able to accept instruction from women is something a lot of men have a problem with, even if they love you. Actually for some of them, *especially* if they love you, as they have a primordial need for you to admire them. Hence you cannot possibly be superiorly skilled and able to give them advice—me Tarzan, you Jane!

You have no idea how much you will learn, and what those things will be. The on-site roles will become more clearly defined as time goes on. Allow each other the space to grow. Are you the more competent of the two of you? Then, bite your tongue and don't be overly critical or say 'that's not how you do it'. Think diplomacy with touchy spouses, otherwise you might find they lose heart.

My then husband once agreed to strip the paint off some windows using a heat gun. I had done so many, and learned what I considered the best way, that I wanted to tell him how to do it. He got really touchy at me correcting him and said, 'Right, I'm not doing anything ever again.' A bit like my cooking really, where I bailed out simply because he was so good. I was amazed though, at how such a neat man could be such a sloppy painter. Is that like someone doing the dishes once and breaking a third of them, so that they're never asked again? If you don't want to do something, say so and say why. Once you start to lose your lines of communication it can be hard to open them up again. A small white lie now can lead to some bigger ones later.

Learn to learn from each other, to accept advice and to give it. One of you will be much better at laying pipes; the other will be a better organizer, a neater painter or a stronger lifter.

Are you a novice working with an experienced partner? Then be attentive and grateful as you have a free teacher. However, I'm sure he doesn't know everything. There will be a slice of the project that you can make exclusively your area of expertise. Does your partner know how to paint fake marble for the fireplace? Strap down roofs? Do leadlight? Paving? Install irrigation? Remove salt damp? You go ahead and learn something of your own that you can be proud of. Take a course, read some books.

Always remember to admire each other, and never knock the other's work. When you have visitors, exclaim about the other's prowess! Sincere flattery is free and greases many cogs, very much like the positive reinforcement in dog training.

A QUESTION OF STYLE

A big source of potential conflict is your individual tastes. Do they complement each other? If you have the best-developed sense of aesthetics you might have the strongest voice, but are you building a house that your partner will feel part of if he has no say? My thoroughly wise mother warned me of this. My then husband didn't contribute to style at all. I'd ask his opinion and he would mumble something absent-mindedly and I'd then forge ahead. I didn't even know if he hated anything. When it came to deciding on the colour of the house, I had visualized all along that it would be a pale yellow; it was just how I *knew* the house in my head. I had the colour chart in front of me admiring the tint I'd selected. It was a bit lighter than I'd wanted, but it changed with the light from a chalky cream to a warm yellow depending on the time of day. I was happy with that. I showed my husband the chart and said, 'What do you think?'

He pointed to a terracotta red and said, 'That's the best one.'

My heart did strange little protesting flutters and I said, 'No, this one would be great.'

He replied, 'What did you ask me for then if you've already made up your mind?'

I knew then that the whole house would end up being terracotta. And it did… and the house looks *pink*! I hated it for a long time but have grown to tolerate it now, even like it. Sadly, I think it was already too late for our relationship by then.

Peruse magazines together, tear pictures out and discuss them. Have a bookshop morning, hang out in the style section and if you see the books you need to get you going, buy them. They can be very expensive but will be worth it a thousand times over. Then go out for coffee, reading your brand new style manuals. You may not be aware of what kind of house he is dreaming of; you might even assume it looks the same as yours. There are elements I would have wanted to include in the house but didn't in order to maintain peace; but each time I was surprised that my husband didn't share

If you want to keep your relationship and doubt that it could survive building, *don't build together*. It is much, much easier to build solo than to jolly along a reluctant spouse. This way you have no worries except where to find that extra set of hands for lifting lintels into place. Having built both with a partner and alone, I would have no hesitation in setting out for a solo build again. You can either treat it as a joint financial project where you are the project manager, or it can be your project in which case you will get autonomy. If this doesn't sound possible for you now, it might in a few years. View it like organizing a business.

my taste. I mean, how could he not?

I was vaguely and briefly seeing someone once who clashed stylistically with me. His house was austerely minimalist, all black and white, with carpet everywhere except the bathroom. As for me, I am a colourful eclectic clutterer with a clinical aversion to wall-to-wall fluffy covering, preferring floors that either creak or go clang. If we had designed a house together it would have had to be like that of the artists Frieda Kahlo and Diego Rivera. They had two sections to their house, connected by a footbridge. Otherwise, I would have gone crazy living his clinically bare life, and he would not have coped with my mess.

Honestly, you need to put some effort into the issue of style. A couple I know had a house built, and he let her decorate it since she would be home all day with the children while he worked. She made it all lilac, her favourite colour. The carpets were mauve with lavender walls, and the tiles looked like the leftover cream in the bottom of a bowl of blueberries. The sofa blended right in! You only realized something was amiss when you looked at his office. It was a sanctuary of murky browns and creaky leather, reminiscent of a fine city gentleman's club. If that was his natural preference, how did living in the house make him feel? Quite sick, probably. All he had was his one-room dark refuge of tobacco tints. Could not some compromise have been reached, where both could indulge their tastes? Imagine waking up every day to a violet lace canopy when you'd prefer a mellow hunting scene…

Here are some light-hearted questions that might help you to uncover any potential style clashes.

- Is the local pub the epitome of style or was Queen Victoria the quintessential style mogul?

- Is a dead elephant foot a suitable and dignified receptacle for umbrellas?

- Does orange Laminex nauseate you? Is vinyl flooring OK or is flagstone the only option?

- Do you need to incorporate car memorabilia in the design or cover the building in shells?

- Are flying duck silhouettes kitsch or stylish?

- Do you share the same passion for Jugend, fin-de-siècle or post-modern Finnish architecture?

I leave this line of questioning for you to explore, just make sure you do. You can live with someone for a long time and not know them. Did your partner live by himself before you decided to join forces? That could give you an indication of his style, but not necessarily. He might have a stash of secret dreams…

Taste and style are qualities you learn and develop. Study together; talk about how you experience houses you visit. If your styles differ greatly, perhaps you could both learn to appreciate something totally different. All that matters is for the two of you to love the home you're making.

MONEY AND HOW TO SPEND IT

Did you go on overseas holidays, spend weekends away, have dinner out, or buy clothes? Unless you have huge coffers, you will probably find you have little spare cash as building and renovating use up all the money you can find, and still leave you short. I can easily fall into the trap of not spending *any* money except on the house. Please don't do that. Set some money aside to do things together that take you away from the site occasionally.

A weekend away sometimes is a great idea. Small, regular inexpensive things like walks, movies, live music, dinners, dog training classes and dancing are also good to do. These are things that don't take too much time or money. You don't have to do the same things of course, but if only one of you has leisure activities you could be in trouble again. The person who keeps working on the house while the partner enjoys 18 holes of golf might feel some pretty strong resentment. Meet halfway, and be prepared to negotiate. Let building be as much fun as you can. Include and encourage each other.

THE ACHIEVEMENT OF SUCCEEDING

As you reach goal after goal, climbing that metaphorical mountain, you will feel tremendous. As a couple building together, that achievement is yours to share. Let your hearts soar with the joy of your success! Celebrate small milestones. There will be many opportunities. Have a special party for when the roof is finally up. In Sweden we make a wreath with leaves and flowers, put it up on the roof and have what's known locally as *taklagsöl*, meaning 'a roof team beer', where you invite everyone who helped. Make merry when the foundations have been poured with a formal dinner—white linen and all—straight on the slab. Have a three-course dinner delivered. Dance naked in order to properly celebrate lock-up (maybe skip this one if you have curious neighbours). Have a grand occasion for the first shower with running water. Why waste the opportunity to create special events and celebrate?

IF IT DOESN'T WORK OUT

What happens if, in spite of all the romantic concrete laying and wheel-barrowing, you decide to break up? Well, when you have finished crying and decided that it's irrevocably over, you'll need to think about the money side. Not only will you have a broken relationship to be emotional about, but you will also have the additional responsibility of the house.

If at all possible, you could try to make a pact to finish it. Or, if you can find any extra money, you could pay for builders to finish it for you—perhaps it is

worth asking the bank for assistance. That way you will be able to sell the house for more, as an incomplete house is usually worth not much more than the land value. Not many people want someone else's building site and it is far harder to sell than just land.

In a court settlement, they will look at how you got to where you are, who contributed what financially, who worked on the house, and who 'owns' the biggest portion. Bear the six-year rule in mind, too (see page 53). I ended up keeping the house, through a variety of personal circumstances that possibly won't apply to many people. Every situation is different. You might feel you just want to get rid of the house quickly, as there is so much pain involved and you want a clean slate. I strongly advise against acting too rashly, as you could change your mind after the pain has abated. I didn't know what to do except to finish my house. Angus had been waiting for so long to have his room; we had been talking about the pool getting water in it, how strong the jets would be, the sleepover he would be allowed to have once his room was done, and so on. Could I stamp on his already crushed heart? No, I couldn't. And so, we stayed put.

Think about all your options and write them down. If it seems like you only have one single option, ask other people. There are usually other paths you can't see. We become blind to our situation. I remember one afternoon, sitting in the kitchen contemplating life, the universe and everything. Suddenly I felt like I had been hit by an electrical charge and I clearly saw several very good options. Let your brain work in peace, and it might find a path for you to follow. Keep putting one foot in front of the other and you'll be OK…

I hope that after reading this chunky section you'll be confident enough to have a go at the practical side of your project. I'll give you my opinion on how hard or not things can be, as well as show you how to keep your offspring safe and happy, and give you a crash course in self-preservation.

5

SKILLS AND TOOLS

IN WHICH WE LEARN WHY WE NEED AN ANGLE GRINDER AND WHERE TO FIND THE 'HOW-TO'

It is extremely important to understand that you don't need to know everything straight away. It's just plain unnecessary. What you need is a general overview, and then you'll learn how to do each process as it's needed. Don't worry too much about the specifics now.

BUILDING YOUR SKILLS

If you can read, half the battle is won. You are skilling up right at this moment. There is a publication on everything, so visit your library or bookshop and fill a bag. Your council has information leaflets that may apply to you, and the hardware store often gives out free brochures explaining how to do different jobs. Cooking is made comprehensible through cookbooks, ditto with terrazzo tiling or wallpapering. A little bit of theory goes a long way. Things will soon become more familiar, and the familiar is no longer as intimidating.

Experiment

If you have little experience with tools and their usage, scrounge around for rubbish you can play with. Ask friends if you can have the warped timber that's been lying in their garage for the last decade. See what happens if you drill like this, join like so, or saw like that. You don't need to feel nervous as the material is of no importance. Just read the section on safety first if you are going to use power tools.

When I was twelve I wanted to learn sewing. There was no one in my neighbourhood with any skill, so my grandmother gave me a box of scrappy fabric I could play around with (this also made me stop cutting up the family linen) and I nagged my parents into buying a machine. By the time I had finished experimenting, I could sew reasonably well.

Make something small

To get you started, try making a really simple piece of furniture (a three-legged stool is a good start as three legs *always* remain stable), a garden seat, toys and dollhouses, perhaps a rabbit hutch, mailbox or dovecot. A lidless box is fairly easy to build and serves as a warming up exercise—it gives you confidence to move on to other things. Everything you make is giving you more skills. Different tools and techniques will be needed and you gain greater understanding of the processes involved. Plus, you can make your mistakes small on small projects! It is not much harder to make

an extension to your house than a box for the CD collection; the most important difference is your mindset. You just have to believe me.

Visit other people's projects

There are plenty of people around already doing similar things to what you want to do. Find them and ask if you can spend a day or a weekend helping. Since you are offering free labour, you might be very welcome as an aid to a poor tired renovator or builder. A couple of women laid bricks with me for a few days. It was fun to have company and we surged ahead. Maybe you will come to the realization that you don't want to do it like that at all, which is an invaluable lesson. Offer your help properly, don't just come to ask questions. If you are asked to carry bricks for hours do so willingly; give the weekend up to them and your answers will emerge as you go. Write down your key issues in advance, and take note of the solutions.

If you have no friends to visit, place an advertisement specifically stating what kind of work you're interested in. There are magazines dedicated to people renovating and building. Ask around. Advertise on notice boards. Ask at your local hardware if they know of anyone. You could try asking the council, too.

For peace of mind for your hosts, given the current public liability concerns, you could provide a waiver stating that you will take full responsibility for any personal injuries. Do observe safety when you are on another site, and don't do anything rash or silly. It will make your hosts nervous.

Courses

Adult education offers handy short courses on skills from bricklaying and leadlight to longer programs on all issues involving owner-building. You can take whole term courses in welding or woodwork, or weekend workshops dealing with specific issues like salt damp. If you live in a rural area or you're home with young children it can be hard to get out and do these things. Don't worry, a book is often as useful and can be read at home without the

need to pay for babysitters or travel for long hours. The only drawback is that you won't get to try things hands-on or have the opportunity to ask questions. Find someone else to ask!

Get a mentor

If you have a friend with greater knowledge than you ask if they want to be your 'over-the-phone-panic-helper'. I have a guy who fields my queries whenever I call, stressed and breathless, wanting to know how to fix something that isn't turning out the way it should, or wanting to know which way is up when I'm laying insulation. A mentor can be your most valuable support. Perhaps it's a grandparent, the man down the street or your cousin in Wagga. Think about it, I'm sure there is someone suitable. Bribe them with the occasional bottle of wine.

A great source for finding mentors if you don't know anyone is in a senior citizen's club. You could advertise for one through newsletters published by associations such as the Council on the Aging (COTA). All tradespeople and other handy folk have to retire eventually and someone will surely welcome you as their protégé. It doesn't really matter where they live, unless you want direct supervision, and it's lovely to have someone to bounce ideas off. Do they think this or that would work? Why? Why not?

Go out and look at building sites, and learn from them. In order to work confusing things out I have stickybeaked at timber framing, roofing, and guttering. So that's how they do it…

Internet

Television home shows and hardware chains often have useful Internet sites giving instructions on how to do things. Some have a capacity for answering questions. If you have no mentor to phone, try this option. The problem is the time delay; you probably want an answer immediately as you're likely to be in the middle of something tricky but you may have to wait for days. Still useful if you're planning ahead, though!

Ask the hardware store

Try to develop a good relationship with your hardware shop. Find a store, preferably a builder's store, with knowledgeable staff. I had the fortune of having one so good that if they didn't know the answer they would ask customers, who were mostly builders. If your shop gives you incorrect information they will end up costing you money. Change shop. You don't want one that tries to sell you things you don't want or need, or recommends the wrong kind of nails. Be careful, not all of them know as much as they like to think. Look at their customers; you want to shop where the builders do.

You will get to know your favourite staff and listen to them, and they will start to understand what you mean when you talk like you left the stubbies at home and ask for a 'thingy' yet again. I do that all the time. I'm a Very Tiresome Customer but I spend a lot, which makes up for it. If you can avoid it, don't go on the weekend and *never* on a long weekend, as they are too busy and you will grow stressed over how long it's all taking. You are more likely to get good service at a different time.

You might also ask the supplier of your particular type of product for help directly. They should be able to offer brochures and expert advice.

TOOLS AND EQUIPMENT

There are a few skills you can not do without, but if you have those there is nothing you can't do. You need the patience to measure accurately, to read instructions, and the ability to use a saw, a drill and a hammer. Everything else is a bonus. Like cooking, ensure you have all you need around you before you begin and try to keep a tidy workspace. Make sure you also have the right tools and, with most tools, check that the weight suits you. Sometimes a bigger tool is the best practical option, but if it's going to be too heavy for you to use comfortably, it's no good. Buy something you can handle or you won't be happy using it. Below is an outline of most of the tools and equipment, in alphabetical order, that you're likely to need.

Angle grinder

This is great for making firework effects in the dark! Wear goggles, ear protection, long sleeves and pants, and don't set fire to anything as you create beautiful showers of red-hot sparks, hot enough to burn holes in your clothes.

There are three kinds of blades: one for grinding down things like welds and axe sharpening, one for metal cutting, and one for masonry. You can cut bricks, tiles, metal rods and sheets, whatever. This is a tool I believe you will need. They are cheap, too, but burn out quickly if stressed with a lot of masonry cutting. I have worn out three during my construction, but perhaps if I had bought better quality that wouldn't have happened. If you can afford the very best the first time around you will probably only need to buy once.

A few different sizes are available; a medium one is the most useful but I only have the smallest. I was too scared at the time to plunge in straight away and buy a 'big' tool.

Bricklaying tools

Bricks, hard as they seem, will snap easily when karate-chopped in the correct spot with a **bolster**. This looks a little like a short heavyset half circle on a handle. You place the flat bit on the brick, give the handle a sharp whack with a hammer, turn the brick, do it again, and continue until you have done all four sides of the brick. It will then simply snap, making you feel very powerful!

You also need a **trowel**. Every second garage sale seems to have one on offer. I have two small ones. One was too pointy and I hated it, so I bought another, more rounded one that I love. Then my friend the mason said, 'You'll never get anywhere with that little trowel', so I bought a big one. I now use the big one for raking the ashes from my pizza oven, as I can't possibly build with it. It is far too heavy for me when it's laden with mortar! I needed to hang on to my wussy girly-sized one.

In order to keep the brick courses level, you'll need a **stringline**, which comes in a roll. You also need something to hold the stringline at each end. I prefer the **plastic stringline moulds** that you wind the stringline on and then put on each corner. This draws the stringline so tight that tension alone holds it up. Buy two pairs so you don't have to change walls all the time. My bloody dog ran away with one of mine, never to be seen again (the plastic, not the dog), so I had to buy another set. Fortunately, they're inexpensive.

Cement mixer

Are you going to build using traditional mortar or concrete? If so, buy a cement mixer as it'll be a good investment. I never did; instead I hired and borrowed over various periods of time. Overall, I might as well have bought one and resold it afterwards.

Have a talk with your hardware store before tackling jobs for the first time. They should be able to give useful tips. If they can't, change hardware shop. Buy quality if you can with all tools that you plan to use often. It will make such a difference in durability and finish.

Don't try to mix concrete in a wheelbarrow unless you only have a tiny bit to do. It will kill your back, as all the little rocks in the concrete make it unbelievably heavy. You should aim to stay off the chiropractor's bench. When you mix in a mixer, start by running some water along the edge. This keeps it clean and prevents the mix from getting stuck on the bottom. Pretend you're mixing a cake. To clean the mixer afterwards, let it go around with just the rocks and water in it.

I love concrete. In fact, I paved around my house with it. Sounds awful, I know, but it's not. I laid red bricks in a diagonal checker pattern and filled the squares with concrete. I saved thousands, plus I didn't have to level the ground as thoroughly as you do when you pave. I also rendered my bathroom floor with pale concrete tinted with yellow oxide, then smoothed it with a steel trowel.

Clamps

There are loads of clamps in the shops. However, I did most of my cutting with my foot placed on whatever I was working on, holding it steady with my weight. It is a very quick-release method—simply lift foot! I did buy a **pipe clamp**, which is a piece of threaded pipe cut to length with a clamp at each end. This allows you to clamp really big things, like a whole door, a table or a metre of warped flooring. I also like to keep a couple of **quick-release clamps** around for fast, easy access. It does help with saw safety if you can hold things down properly. Don't buy ones that are time-consuming to use, even if they're cheaper, as you will only get annoyed in the long run.

Drills

There are many types of drill available. If you want to drill into brick, stone or concrete you need a **hammer drill**. It can be used like an ordinary drill, but also has a hammer setting which pounds while it drills. I recommend getting a hammer drill as sooner or later you'll need it.

A **cordless drill** is very handy. It won't always have the same power as an electric one, but it's great for working in a remote location such as up on the roof. You don't actually need one, but it will certainly make some things easier. Imagine struggling up on the roof, hammer between the teeth, drill squeezed between the knees. As you get to the top, the cord unplugs itself because it's snagged on something…annoying! Don't succumb to the temptation of tying the cords together. Though everyone seems to do this, it isn't safe. There are products in the shops especially made to connect two cords.

The following are a few tips to make your drilling easier:

- When you drill into timber, place a piece of scrap wood flat against the spot where the drill bit will come through. This will prevent ugly splintering at the point where the drill bit emerges.

- Drill slowly when drilling holes in metal to avoid burning out the drill bit.

- For drilling large holes, start with a smaller bit, and then increase the drill bit size.

- Masonry bits are recognizable, as their heads are flattish. They are not to be used for drilling wood. When you buy them you'll notice their ends have been dipped in colour to differentiate them from timber bits, but that wears off with the first use.

- When drilling through slippery metal, it helps to make a dent with a pointy punch and a hammer first to avoid the drill slipping and making swirly scratches. When drilling through shiny and slippery tiles, try a bit of tape on the tile.

- Get a full set of screwdriver inserts for the drill. This is by far the best way to do screws!

- Phillips head bits damage wood far less than slotted head bits. The drill bit is likely to slip when you drive in screws and you want to minimize the damage. See for yourself!

Hammer

This is your most important tool, as a bad one will be no help to you at all and there'll be a thousand occasions when you need to use one. The bargain bins at the hardware shop are full of cheap ones you don't want to waste any money on. Try several hammers out first, and get one that feels right in your hand. It needs to feel nicely balanced with good grip. If it's too light you won't get the right swing, and too heavy will wear you out. Where you hold the hammer is important too. Women tend to hold the hammer closer to the head, and men hold it where it's designed to be held. It's true! I think this is a confidence issue—you have to trust that the hammer will land where you want it to even if you hold it further down the handle. If you have good hand-eye coordination it will help. I have very little; I cannot catch balls for instance. A carpenter looked at me driving in a nail once and said, 'Well, at least you have a good hammer...' How patronizing!

The following are some handy hints that will help to get you on friendly terms with your hammer.

- To avoid splitting timber, tap the point of the nail with the hammer to make it blunt. This seems to work, but I don't know why…

- Try to use nails long enough to put two-thirds of their length into the second piece of timber.

- For extra strength, try skew nailing, which basically means you are nailing on an angle.

- If timber splits, you might have to pre-drill as the nails are too thick. Some timber is too hard to nail into without drilling first, like old hardwoods. As the settlers of Australia said, 'Timber like iron, stone like butter.'

- For outside work, use a galvanized nail or it will soon rust.

- There is a nail for every occasion—use the right one. Bullet-headed nails can be countersunk in wood but won't hold composite material, which needs a flat head, and so on. Ask the hardware if you're unsure.

Jigsaw

Get one. A jigsaw is fun, useful and cheap to buy. With the correct blades, you can cut metal or wood and you'll find you invent uses for it. Just make sure you don't position your face directly over it as you work, especially if you are the kind of person who keeps your tongue between your teeth for concentration. I am, and as the jigsaw kicked up in recoil once I nearly bit my tongue off.

Angus as a toddler was once found running around the garden pulling the jigsaw by the cord like a pull-along toy. It had become totally caked with dirt in all the air holes, as it bounced and dangled behind him. Kids! I cleaned it up and I still use this old cheap unit—they make even the budget ones tough.

Miscellaneous hand tools

Buy hand tools as required. If you have a good relationship with your hardware store they might lend you tools for free. Chances are they know you as a good spender and won't mind being nice. This is really useful for one-off jobs. I have over time borrowed an enormous drill bit, a fence tightener, a copper-pipe scorer and a staple gun. However, if you can't borrow, it may be better to buy rather than struggle on with the wrong tool for the job.

My favourite revelation was the special cutter that scores Hardiflex or Villaboard. I used to cut that noxious stuff with a circular saw, churning out the dust, ruining my lungs and hair (though I always wore a mask), and quickly blunting the expensive saw blade. I didn't know there was a better way until I found the cutter. This dust-free method means I now simply score along the cutting line, then fold the board. It snaps instantly!

Planer

If you will be using recycled timber, an electric planer is for you. Otherwise, it's an unnecessary luxury. I have one, but only really use it with old timber. If you need to shave down a door for instance, you might as well sand or saw it down instead of planing. A hand planer could do, unless you are planning to work a lot with this type of material. If you decide to buy an electric one, specify that you want good ball bearings. Poor quality bearings fill with dust and will cause the planer to seize unless replaced. They are not cheap, so it's better to spend a little more now on the best quality bearings to avoid frequent repairs later.

Router

You can do without a router, but it may be useful if you make your own windows and doors and other joinery. I have two: a cheapie that I got many years ago which I hardly ever use, and an expensive one that I mostly use for furniture making. The bits are expensive, and you can always buy readymade mouldings for pretty edges instead.

Sander

There are many options available. The hardware shops try to make you buy one for sanding round things, one for large things, one for balustrades, etc. Find one that suits your needs and that you feel comfortable with. In the interests of economy I have used **orbital sanders** for years. Since winning my *Better Homes and Gardens* prize I am now the proud owner of a nice **belt sander** as well. It collects dust in a dinky little bag and is far superior. I love it.

Saws

There is literally a saw for every occasion. A **circular saw** is necessary if you plan to do any timber work; they come in a variety of sizes. My first circular saw was a very good brand, but the smallest size I could find as the bigger ones looked unnecessarily big and scary. I still have it, and it works well 12 years later. I eventually needed a bigger one, and bought a budget brand as I was low on money. It lasted three months before it simply seized. I got it replaced but it's still useless. The alignment is out, it rattles, it sometimes won't start properly, and I hate it. With circular saws, you truly get what you pay for. I have since splurged on another really expensive one, only bigger. You can immediately feel and see the difference. The only thing I can't cut is laminates, as they chip unless you have a table saw. If you are keen on laminated chipboard, hardware stores can cut it to size for you on their whizz-bang machinery. In fact, your hardware store or timber merchant will cut anything exactly to size for a small fee. They may even waive the fee if you are a good customer. This is a good way for the novice to ease into carpentry!

If you are really interested in fine carpentry and you have pots of gold, I recommend a table-mounted circular saw set-up. You will get exceptional accuracy, and you won't need a mitre saw.

If you have a lot of dust in the air, a few squirts of water from a spray bottle will settle it. The water collects on the dust particles, increasing their weight and causing them to fall.

I rate the basic circular saw as your number two tool, after the hammer. Get the best you can afford.

Be prepared for saws that kick back (fly backwards in a sharp jerky 'kick' movement). If you are aware that this can happen, you will make sure that you stand with both feet firmly on the ground, hold on to the saw firmly, and position the material you're working on correctly. The main reason for kickback is the wood closing in on the cut, jamming the blade. Wood that is properly supported is less likely to do this (see 'Clamps' on page 71).

Handsaws come in a range of shapes and sizes. Fretsaws, tenon saws, little handheld things for sawing round holes…the list goes on. Buy as you go; you won't need that many, especially if you have an electrical jigsaw and a circular saw.

A **mitre saw** is a circular saw mounted on a stand that you can lever to get perfect mitres every time. I love this tool for its ease of use, but I still don't own one—I've never allowed myself the luxury. Instead, I have made do all these years with different manual mitre boxes and a handsaw. My last kitchen had over 200 metres (650 feet) of mouldings in it, and it was all cut by hand. I built some biceps with that job! My present kitchen is free of mouldings.

Set square

Buy a big metal angle—it is an essential tool. Mine's been so well used over the years that the numbers are wearing out. If you need to measure out a right angle on the ground, for setting out bricks when you first start for instance, your set square will be too small. Instead use a tape measure and this ratio, courtesy of Pythagoras: 3:4:5.

This means that if you measure 3 metres along one wall and 4 metres along the next one, the diagonal should be 5 metres if the walls are truly square. Adjust until it is. As this is a ratio, it works for all linear measurements, metric and imperial. So if you measure 3 feet along one wall and 4 feet along another, the diagonal will be 5 feet if the walls are square. Magic!

Spirit level

Don't buy a short one as size matters! Buy a good quality metre-long (3 foot) one for all construction work. It will also double as a long straightedge, and you will find you use it all the time. A spirit level is expensive but it is indispensable as nothing will be level otherwise.

You might also need a long section of clear hose for levelling long distances. When you need to check that all four corners of a room are growing at the same rate, or two ends of a pergola for instance, you can't do without it.

Tape measure

A regular cheapie is fine, but I wouldn't bother buying a short one, I never leave my tape measures out overnight as they can rust, and I expect to replace them occasionally as they wear out. I also recommend that you buy a manual wind-up one for measuring long distances.

Tarpaulin

Get one now so it's ready for when you need it, and buy a big one. I was too poor, and used orange building plastic instead. This is not as good, as it breaks down with exposure to sunlight and you end up with millions of small orange plastic fragments spreading on the wind.

You need a tarpaulin for that sudden rainstorm when materials have just been delivered, and to protect floors or furniture inside from damage, etc.

Tiling tools

Glazed wall tiles will snap after being scratched with a **scorer**, but you need to hire a **cutter** for the floor tiles. The glue is spread with a **notched spreader**—a big notch for the floor and a smaller notch for wall tiles. I have made some spreaders myself by cutting leftover metal with my tinsnips. Don't use too big a notch as tile adhesive is expensive and not to be used in excess. For grouting you will need a **rubber spreader**.

Tool belt

If you are going to do construction carpentry, a tool belt is great. Without it you have nowhere for the tools and nails you need to carry with you. I used to have nails in my pockets, but if I put them in my breast pocket they'd all fall out with a merry tinkle when I bent down. If I put them in my pants pocket, they'd hurt and I couldn't get them out easily, especially if my legs were bent. Go the belt!

Welder

There are different kinds of welder, but the easiest to use is a **MIG welder**. Sadly, a MIG welder is more expensive than a common **arc welder**. A welder may not be on top of your list of essentials as most projects have little call for welding, but it does give very satisfactory results.

I covet a good quality MIG welder. However, if you only need the occasional piece welded, ask almost anyone with a shed if they have one and you shouldn't be surprised to find an old arc welder in there. Be careful not to look without the black visor though, as you *will* injure your eyes.

Wheelbarrow

For building work, you'll need a nice deep wheelbarrow. Little fiddly garden barrows will just become annoying when you start building. If your barrow clogs up with dry mortar because you don't clean it properly, don't worry. When the mortar is thick enough, whack it with a hammer and it will all crack and fall off.

A WORD TO THE OLDER WOMAN

The world is full of widows, as we so often outlive our male partners. We may find ourselves one day standing in a shed full of tools we don't even know the name of, never mind what they're used for. Don't be too hasty in disposing of them all or letting the tools so painstakingly collected over a lifetime get divvied up between the relatives. You might find you enjoy

learning how to fix and make stuff yourself; in fact, there could be a new world waiting to be explored.

You are now in the interesting situation of owning all the tools you could ever need and then some, unlike younger women who will only own a hammer and a screwdriver if they are lucky, and have to prioritize their needs. Did you spend your life having things done for you? Maybe now you can put up the proverbial shelf yourself. You might surprise yourself and enjoy it. Just because you've never done something doesn't mean that you can't. Many women, like me, have waited for a man to come home and do the drilling for them. Why not take charge of your situation and the mysterious contents of your fabulous shed? You could find yourself and your new skills in hot demand amongst your friends!

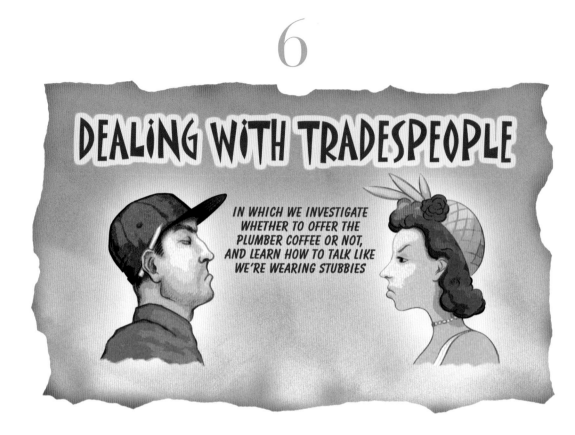

6

DEALING WITH TRADESPEOPLE

IN WHICH WE INVESTIGATE WHETHER TO OFFER THE PLUMBER COFFEE OR NOT, AND LEARN HOW TO TALK LIKE WE'RE WEARING STUBBIES

Frankly, does anyone know how to deal with tradespeople? Many of them look upon owner-builders with poorly concealed loathing, and women owner-builders are viewed with a good measure of incredulity as well. I once had a tradesman pinch my waist just to check if I 'had any fat'! I dislike making generalizations like this but many grains of truth fill a whole silo. Half of my tradesmen have been smashing guys, the rest not. You need to stay sharp to keep on top of them. Be professional and respectful in your approach to them, and hope they will return the courtesy.

SUBCONTRACTING

You can be an owner-builder without even chipping your nail polish. If you employ a general builder, he will provide you with the know-how and bullying power to coordinate all the trades needed for your project. In return for being in charge, he will bill you a percentage of the total sum. He will know all the available tradesmen, and have people he hires regularly.

However, with a little knowledge and a stubborn streak you can quite easily do his job and save a bundle. You will need to be very assertive, though, in order to take control. Be prepared to tolerate bullying and/or patronizing.

As soon as you are ready to lodge your plans with the council, find some contractors and book them. This way you can keep them posted on how your approval is coming along, and they'll be prepared for you when you say 'go'. You'll find some tradespeople are very heavily booked up in advance!

CHOOSING A TRADESPERSON

First, you will need to get quotes, preferably at least three. Make sure each quote covers exactly the same thing. Put what you want done in writing, and photocopy one for each tradesperson you've asked to quote. Don't hand out your large nice expensive blueprints. It is unlikely an unsuccessful bidder for the job will bother to return them, and neither will the successful one, as he will wear it out. Make multiple copies of your blueprints and hand out the relevant sections only.

Find out the availability of each tradesperson, and how much notice they require. Then treat it as a guideline only, as lots of tradespeople are impossible to pin down to a time. Bad weather can cause big delays, better paying urgent jobs might get offered, the salmon are running…who knows? I'm sure some give totally wrong times on purpose, in order to keep all the jobs in the air. No other group of people gets away with this dreadful behaviour. If you go to your dentist's appointment, he doesn't tell you to come back in a week, or perhaps after Christmas at the earliest because he just got busy with someone else. Why is there a whole group of competent

If you are building a house from scratch, the general order of things is roughly as follows (depending on your chosen building technique of course):

STAGE OF BUILDING	SUBCONTRACTOR REQUIRED
Site preparation (this includes demolition, drainage and earthmoving)	earthmover
Dig for foundations	concreter
Electricity, plumbing and phone lines (in ground)	electrician, plumber, Telstra
Termite protection	pesticide company
Foundations, slab	concreter, bricklayer
Walls	carpenter, bricklayer, etc
Roof	carpenter and roofing contractor
Electricity, telephone and plumbing in walls	electrician, plumber
Doors (lock-up—yippee!)	carpenter
Line the walls and ceilings	Gyprocker, plasterer, etc
Line the floor	tiler, carpenter, etc
All second fix (woodwork detail, architraves, skirting boards, etc)	carpenter
Plumbing & electricity	plumber & electrician
Telephone	electrician with a telephone licence (not all have one)
Kitchen	cabinetmaker, kitchen supplier
Painting	painter

Personally, I also recommend paving around the house as soon as the walls are done to avoid dragging dirt through the house and to protect the foundations from water damage.

adults out there with no concept of time? I have found a couple of people who showed up when they said they would, but there's usually a catch. Some show for ten minutes and go away again, not to be seen for two weeks. It's a bad joke!

Hire people you like. After all, you will be spending time with them *and* giving them all your money. Some may try to rip you off, so be cautious. I want to believe the best of people, always, but the reality is that there are plenty of scheming, shortcutting, rude, slimy bastards out there who want much money for little or inferior work.

Beware of a tradesperson offering a cash price. One of the main reasons to be cautious is that you will have no legal standing if anything goes wrong with the job.

CONTRACTS

When you have found your tradespeople, you will need to agree to a formal contract if you are doing it by the book. I have been down this road many times and the trades often refuse to comply. Many of them have never signed a contract in their lives and will ask why you can't simply work on trust or the quote. They seem unwilling to enter into a contract, and I am always uncomfortable trying to pin people down. I'm afraid they will walk off the job… However, at the very least, you should try to get contracts for the biggest and most important jobs. My swimming pool concreters were the only ones that offered a written guarantee!

A simple contract should include the following:

◆ the date

◆ your name and details

◆ the contractor's name and details

◆ exactly what work the contractor is employed to do

◆ the agreed price

◆ any council restrictions on allowable working hours

◆ all insurance details

- the agreed completion date for the work and any penalties imposed in the event of a delay

- who is responsible for scaffolding (scaffolding has its own set of regulations)

- whether the contractor is required to clean up

- that any damage caused will be made good by the contractor, including damage to the work of any other trades

- that all work is to be done to Australian Standards

- the period for which defects are covered.

There may be other clauses you would like to include—do so, as long as they are legal! Once drawn up, the contract should be signed, witnessed and dated by both you and the contractor.

I haven't always had a contract myself, and have been lucky not to hit any major trouble. But when the concreter wants to charge you a bit extra because the plumbers' trenches removed so much dirt that he needed to order more concrete than he'd specified, a contract will help you to determine who is responsible. If you have enough foresight (and determination!) to provide everyone with a contract, you will be better covered against all eventualities.

ORGANIZING YOUR SCHEDULE

If you are a good and organized builder, you will write a list of all the trades required—in their correct order—including any jobs you are considering doing yourself. You can then work out what materials you need to get, and when you're going to need them. Next it's time to sit back and think about money. You don't have to have all your building money ready at once, but it's good if you have a rough idea of when you're going to need funds available, and how much you'll require.

For example, I planned to receive a delivery of bricks in March and then another one in June. This meant I'd need to find about $1700 in time for each delivery. Budgeting in this way makes the project manageable and

prevents you from thinking about the grand total too much. Know that unless you build a cubbyhouse, it will be hideously expensive. You never talk in hundreds of dollars; it's always thousands…or tens of thousands.

Below is an example of a simple planner.

JOB	TRADE	ME	MATERIAL NEEDED	ESTIMATED COST	TIME-FRAME	CALLED TRADE
Prepare walls in bathroom		✓	Timber, Hardiflex, damp-proofing, nails, screws	$300	1/6	
Tile shower		✓	Tiles, glue, grout	$420	10/6	
Plumb in new shower	Plumber		Fit the shower & floor drain	$190	15/6	9/5 ✓ confirm on 10/6

As you go you can make a more precise, separate list of the materials you'll need. If you can guess approximately how much each stage will cost, include that, but don't be alarmed when the money runs out too fast. As I've said before, I started with very little and let money build up as I carried on with what I had in the meantime. Do you have anything you can sell? My saxophone went in favour of bits and pieces. Have a clean-out. Will you really still want that old sofa, fridge or washing machine when you move into the newly built or renovated house?

GETTING YOUR SUBCONTRACTOR TO SHOW UP

Being in charge of subbies is a complex time-management exercise. If they come to work on a site that is not yet ready for them, you will be paying them for nothing and making them grumpy as well. However, if they are not there on time, they will delay the next trade you have already booked in and you are—again—in trouble. It's horrible. It's stressful. It's…subcontracting!

If your subcontractors give you a date, make sure it is written in both of your diaries. Tell them you will call and confirm a few days before that they're still on track. Call them the night before as well. You should also check in the morning that they have showed up. You could consider offering a bonus (or

a penalty) to make sure they're at your site when they promised. Hassle them to get them to your site, but not once they're there!

If your contractor really doesn't want to show up, there's little you can do to make him. However, if you have a contract, at least you have the law on your side. Beyond that, I have discovered a couple of basic tactics that may or may not help you if your contractor goes missing.

The phone is your friend

I once needed some fencing done. It was a hilly job and a little awkward, but not *that* bad. I had started putting posts in myself, but had hurt my wrist from the constant twisting action of the posthole digger, so wanted to pay someone to come with a mechanical one and whack the posts in. There are many vineyards where we live and a few different fencing contractors trawl the area looking for work. I phoned one who came round and looked at the job. He said 'hmm' a lot, but agreed to start in two weeks time, on a Friday, if I could slash the fence line first to make access easy. He thought $1000 was a reasonable sum, including materials, and I agreed. It would take the weekend to put it in.

So I started slashing the fence line with my handheld petrol-powered brushcutter. The first day, to my dismay, the slasher broke, so I tried to get a spare part. Well, that would take two weeks to get in. So I thought I'd hire one. The price for hiring one for four days was equal to buying one so I spent nearly $400 on a new brushcutter, desperate to fulfil my part of the bargain. Then I slashed the line, which took about a week, but no one came on the specified day. I hate chasing people (problems already…) so I thought I'd wait another week. No one came. Then I called and called, but couldn't get an answer for several weeks. When I finally spoke to the contractor, he told me that all his equipment was far up north at the moment and wouldn't be available for another three months. Seething, I called another contractor.

He came, looked at the job, said 'hmm' a few times and declared he would do it. It would take three days and he would charge $1000 per day plus materials. And it would be 'very difficult' to put the posts in behind the

house. The contractors just weren't interested enough in my job to take it on as they could get very good money for whacking in posts in a straight line on flattish ground for the wineries. Six months later when my wrist was better, I put in the posts myself assisted by a good friend. This is one reason people choose to do things themselves—they don't have to deal with tradesmen!

Lesson one: phone your contractor immediately when he doesn't show.

Do what it takes

The first time I renovated, I was befriended by a man who knew various subcontractors. He claimed to be able to get me all kinds of discounts. He recommended a carpenter who would do a good job for reasonable pay, as he had not worked regularly for a while and was in need of some money. I hired him, but soon found that the only way to get him on site was to go to his house at 7 am every day, wake him and then drive him to the site. He had lost his driving licence, I believe, because of a drinking problem. Any advance pay meant he went on a binge and couldn't work at all. He still owes us $100, as he never finished part of the job!

Lesson two: get your tradesperson on site by whatever means you have.

HANDLING YOUR TRADESPEOPLE

What do tradespeople want? On the whole, they just want to do their job when it suits them without any hiccups. They want to know exactly what they are supposed to do, and exactly how much they will get paid in the end. They may want to get paid a bit once they have started the job and the rest after completion. Sounds simple? Perhaps, but if you are to ensure that everything runs smoothly, you'll need to learn to be assertive and stubborn. I regret to say that I am not as assertive as I could be, something amply illustrated by the following story.

I had bought a gorgeous old door, resplendent with a handmade lock and hinges in an antique shop. On the way home, I popped into the blacksmith's, to see if he could make something to fix the hinges.

The blacksmith asked how much I had paid for it. '$70 dollars,' I said.

'I'll give you $90,' said the smithy.

'No.'

'$120?'

'Nope.'

'$140?'

'Sorry, it's just not for sale. But I would love it if you could replace a couple of missing bits.'

Discuss with tradespeople exactly what you want them to do *before* they begin the job, and don't change your mind once they've started.

'Of course,' he said. 'If you take the lock off as well, I'll clean it up for you.'

So I returned with all the bits in a bag and said there was no real hurry.

'Good,' he said. 'I'll phone you when I'm done.'

After maybe two months I phoned him, wondering how it was going. 'Too busy, I'll do it soon.'

Fine. Every few months we'd speak, but there was no progress. Another six months went by, and I needed more work done. I went to see him, as there were no other blacksmiths around at the time. No, the hinges weren't done but he would do my other job fast. A week later, the new job was done, and he felt such remorse over the hinges he charged me embarrassingly little.

'When will the hinges be done?'

'Soon.'

Every few months we'd speak or meet. Once, he feigned amnesia saying he didn't know who I was, then changed his mind. Honestly.

'Have you lost my bag?' I asked.

'No, no. I'll do it.'

He didn't do it until I eventually got *really* angry; then he made them in one day. When I went to pick them up, my boyfriend told me not to pay him as he'd behaved terribly. But that's just not my style—what good would a further petty argument do me? I thought he wouldn't charge, anyway. He handed me the hinges and the lock (not cleaned up), but he had lost all the old screws. The replacements he gave me were all too long and would stick out through the door. I was sick of the whole thing by now.

'That will be $15,' said the smith. 'I didn't charge you very much given the circumstances.'

I opened my wallet without any argument.

'Thanks, you just bought yourself a bottle of wine,' he said, and handed me a great bottle of red in return.

It ended kind of well, but it took nearly three years. How could I have done things differently? Perhaps if I hadn't been so complacent initially, the situation wouldn't have got out of control. Learn from my mistakes and make sure you set a clear timeframe and price at the start of the job.

REDUCING THE COST OF TRADESPEOPLE

There's no doubt that all the money spent on subcontractors adds up quickly. However, if you're wondering where your next cent is coming from, or whether you'll be able to finish your house within the next decade, there are ways you can cut costs.

Supervision

Do you have more time than money? Do you want to do something yourself but aren't sure how to do it properly? Why not hire a semi-retired builder to supervise you. You can put an advertisement in the local news-paper, or on the supermarket noticeboard. Be sure to ask any builders willing to help what your and their legal requirements are, *before* you begin working with them.

Once you've found a supervisor, arrange for them to give you instruction first. They can come and inspect your work at arranged intervals, and finish off anything too tricky or anything requiring qualifications. A poverty-stricken owner-builder can save a lot of money this way. My plumber, a good man, would tell me what to dig, and come back to do the qualified work after I had prepared everything for him. I paid the supplier of my first trusses a bit extra for him to stay for a couple of hours to show me how to erect them. My friend Monica underpinned her house by paying for someone to supervise her. She did her re-wiring the same way. This is a great idea if you can find people who are willing to work with you, as the job gets done properly at a mere fraction of the price!

Exchange of skills

You might have a skill a tradesperson can make use of. What do you do for a living? Could you teach his son to play violin, help his daughter to get better grades in French, or repair his car? Perhaps you could consider a swap. Only once have I done this in regard to building, but it worked well. I made leadlight in exchange for earthmoving services. We both saved money. I have also done leadlight for babysitting, and taught remedial reading for guitar lessons. If you have children in school, the school newsletter can be a good place to advertise your existing skills and those you require.

There may be some tax implications in large-scale bartering, so check with the appropriate authorities first.

MATTERS OF ETIQUETTE

If your tradesperson does something that annoys or upsets you, it can be difficult to know how to handle it. You are within your rights to fire people who behave badly, but you probably wouldn't unless they were jeopardizing safety. I wish I could give you a diplomatic way that works, but I haven't got one. You could perhaps retaliate in kind, or if the thought of that makes you ill, simply go away for the day. I had someone who all day long wouldn't stop swearing at his apprentice ('f-ing stupid, can't you do anything right'), or me ('f-ing owner-builders, don't know how to use a straightedge'), or even my

dog ('f-ing mutt'). It made me feel so uncomfortable that I would go away when he was there, effectively cutting down on time I could have spent building. I wish I could have had the guts to stop him, but I felt I had to tolerate him until he'd finished the job! I pity his apprentices. Apparently, he couldn't keep any of them for long. I wonder why…?

On a more positive note, and assuming you're getting along fine, should you offer your tradesperson coffee? I say yes. You have to hope he won't bill you for the time he sat down, but even if he does, it's still a good way to build rapport. However, keep children away while your expensive tradespeople work, as your kids' chatting will cost you in lost working time. A polite tradesperson will stop and chat with your children, and go to look at whatever they've been asked to, such as an insect with very bright wings. This is expensive, though nice for the kids.

Go so far as to remove your kids and any pets for maximum efficiency. As the trades carry things in and out of the house they might also let things out that should have stayed inside. Have you seen the dog lately? What about the toddler? You should keep out of your tradesperson's way, too! They won't like you breathing down their necks. Visit friends for the day and let the tradespeople get on without you there to hamper progress. Inspect the job after they have gone, but leave them to their work.

THE 'STUBBIE' DICTIONARY

In order to aid your communication with both the hardware store and your tradespeople, why not learn to talk like you're wearing stubbies?*

By learning a few relevant words you will cut a more credible figure with your tradespeople. It will also stop the smirks that come your way if you call everything a plank or a thingy. You might know what you mean, but you're the only one who does. There are plenty more terms, but this is all I have ever needed to know. This is serious stuff—after all, if you use the right words, will they know you don't know anything else?

Barge boards The boards at the end of the gables that finish everything off nicely. They're like fascias but without the guttering.

Caulking Sticky stuff in tubes that seals gaps in buildings. You'll need a caulking gun to apply it.

Collar tie A plank, bolted across the apex of the roof that stiffens up the structure and prevents the roof from pushing the walls out. I have a whole lot in my roof, but it's more common in older buildings.

Control joint (CJ) This is a vertical line in the brickwork which encourages controlled cracking in one spot. You lay a slightly flexible metal tie to act as a bridge across two sections of wall. On the plan this will simply be marked 'CJ'. While it results in a tidier crack, it doesn't stop the cracks from happening.

Conventional roof This is a roof built on site, for which you really need professionals. With a conventional roof you can get a sloped ceiling if you want, but it's more expensive than trusses.

Cornice A nicely shaped profile that covers the gap left between wall and ceiling.

Dampcourse, liquid A chemical additive for mortar to prevent salt damp (also known as rising damp). It is used in conjunction with the DPC.

Damp-proof course (DPC) A special black plastic that you put on a brick course to prevent moisture rising in the wall. It will last a long time unless exposed to sunlight. Called DPC on your plan.

Deflection What normal people call 'sag', except it only refers to timber, not body parts!

Dressed All Round (DAR) As opposed to rough sawn timber. The dimensions of the resulting timber will be slightly smaller as it will have passed through a thicknessing machine. DAR is slightly more expensive. (When going on special outings, I'm DAR in order to conceal any deflections!)

Efflorescence If you see a white mineral build-up that looks like salt crystal on bricks or concrete, it's efflorescence. Do not be alarmed. It isn't rising damp and you can easily remove it with a brush. You should look at what caused the damp, though, to prevent any possible future damage.

Elevation A plan showing your house upright.

Expansion joints These are like control joints, but allow for the wall to really move. You lay a special galvanized thing in the wall, which is like two metal rods on one side sliding into metal pipes on the other. Then you have to add black foam strips to stop the weather from coming in. Now that you know what expansion joints are, you will see them in buildings everywhere. If you plan for your walls to be no longer than 6 metres (20 feet) before taking a turn, you shouldn't need them. No old buildings have them, they just crack freely.

Fascia The long bits of wood that sit behind the gutters and finish off the roof.

First fix All the rough construction carpentry and early plumbing.

Flashing Used in many areas and available in many materials, this is basically a flexible lining that you place around windows and roofs in order to prevent water entering the house.

Frogs This is a depression in old bricks that the mortar should fill in order to create a strong wall. These days, most bricks are made with holes in them instead of frogs. If you are using this kind of brick, the frogs should be laid facing up.

Gang nails or nail plates These are metal plates full of nails. They work like sticky tape for wood. It took me years before I discovered the pleasures of nail plates or gang nails. With them, you don't need to know any fancy joinery techniques in order to do construction carpentry. Simply put the nail plates on both sides of where you want to join your wood for a strong no-budge fastening.

Jambs This is the timber that surrounds the doors. Jambs are most commonly made out of meranti, which is the cheapest hardwood available. You need something harder than pine as otherwise the screws would not stay in.

Joists, ceiling Continuous lengths of timber to which you attach the ceiling.

Joists, floor The big support beams the floors rest on.

Kiln-dried timber Cut-down timber must be dried before you can use it, as it shrinks. It can be seasoned by stacking it, covered, in the open air, or it can be kiln-dried which makes it as dry as can be. Still, before laying kiln-dried floorboards or hanging doors for instance, keep the timber in the house for a few days to allow for it to adapt to your moisture conditions.

Lintels These are supporting structures over your doors and windows that prevent the wall from leaning on them. They can be wood, metal, concrete, etc. You must leave a small gap between the lintel and your window to prevent windows from breaking under any downward pressure later on.

Noggins What a great word! Noggins are short lengths of horizontal timber that get nailed between the upright lengths to brace the wall from wobbling and buckling under the pressure of the roof.

Oregon A common construction timber. I used to think it was the actual name of a specific type of tree, but it really refers to Douglas fir from Oregon in the United States. It used to be stronger than it is these days, as producers now force the trees to grow too quickly, in order to maximize their profits. You may as well use pine, which has about the same moisture resistance.

Parapet Any brickwork higher up than the roof. Not so common these days, parapets can be used to give a fancy appearance to the plainest of designs. Sometimes you will need to build one to blend in with an older streetscape.

Piers The masonry pillars holding up your floor (as opposed to stumps).

Pig A bulge in the brickwork. This is not very desirable, as you can't fix a pig without demolishing and rebuilding the section. However, you can avoid them by paying attention to the stringline.

Purlins The long timbers that run horizontally along the roof, holding it all together.

R2, etc The rating given to insulation. The higher the number, the better the insulation.

Radiata The pine which most timber-framed buildings are made from. It comes in different stress grades for different applications.

Rafters The biggest component of a conventional roof, these are the heavier bits that go from the ridge to the wall. Trussed roofs don't have rafters.

Retarder An additive you can add to concrete if pouring the slab in very hot weather to slow its drying. You can also get a quickset alternative.

Ridge The spine of your roof. You will have a ridge cap on it when the roof is finished.

Sarking The stuff that gets nailed to the roof before the roof covering goes on. It is often a reflective foil.

Second fix The tradespeople's finishing touches: the hanging of doors, the fitting of lights and taps, etc.

Sills The things under the windows that enable the rain to run off.

Skillion roof A roof that only slopes one way, ie. it hasn't got a central ridge.

Soffit This is the bit underneath the roof overhang.

Sparky, chippie, brickie, etc I'm sure I don't need to explain these!

Stress grade of timber You will find mysterious numbers, like F4, written on your plans. These refer to a helpful standardized timber grading system. Your plans may state that your wall plates are to be F7—this will ensure they are strong enough to support your construction. Some hardwoods don't have stress grades, but all pine does. It matters. You can see streaks of paint on the timber, too. Green means F5, blue is F7, and black F11. This way the building inspector can check that you've used the right stuff. If you have built your whole house with the wrong material, you may well have to redo it. Check that you always receive what you've asked for. Obviously, it doesn't matter if the timber is stronger than the required grade.

Struts Timber bits that add support to the roof.

Studs These are the long vertical timbers that support the roof and give you the basis for the walls.

Stumps These are timber supports that hold up the floor (as opposed to piers).

Tie down This is when you strap all your roof timbers to the walls and to each other. It can be done with rods, metal strapping and Tek screws or hundreds of tiny nails. Your plans will specify exactly how many and the size of nail or screw. Make sure you follow this exactly, as there are a couple of slightly different widths of strapping for instance. Before the roof goes on, the council will come out on an inspection to check your tie down, and can make you redo the whole thing if it's not done to specification.

Trusses Pre-made triangles of roof sections. Your ceiling cannot slope, as these are triangles and so have a flat base, but you can have the trusses exposed, which will give added height to your rooms.

Wall plates The long plank-like things on top of your walls that spread the weight of the roof.

Wet trades This refers to all the trades that mix up gooey things from powders and water, like bricklayers and tilers.

*In case you don't know, stubbies are the short shorts favoured by Aussie tradesmen. They come in a range of attractive shades, and were named after a small beer bottle. Of course!

7

The a-z of construction

In which personal opinions are expressed on how hard or not it really is to do nearly everything

If you have an attitude of 'I can', you will find everything easier than if you are already sure that you can't. Perhaps the building industry makes things out to be more difficult to do than they really are so that you don't threaten tradespeople's livelihoods. They shouldn't worry, as most people have no interest whatsoever in tackling anything bigger than changing a light globe. Builders are not short of work at the moment. In fact, they are so busy that you might have to do things yourself in order to get them done at all, especially small jobs. You could spend more time trying to get them on site than you would if you actually did the job yourself.

This chapter runs alphabetically through a lot of the jobs you could encounter in any building or renovation project. I have given every job a rating. Remember that this is my personal opinion; you may disagree. If you are a tradesman and I have said your job is so easy anyone can do it, don't be offended. I know you can do it faster and better. Since I am not, in fact, a builder I have only mentioned the techniques I have experience with. I am sure you'll find you're able to tackle most jobs, with patience and practice, as long as you have the confidence to try. For detailed technical information you will need to consult more indepth books.

	Easy
	Moderate
	Reasonably tricky
	Very tricky
	Don't mess with it

Built-in furniture

Rating: and up

Anything built-in is a great beginner's project, especially if it doesn't have doors. You don't need the same stability in something that will be attached to a wall as you do with freestanding units. Built-in wardrobes, bookcases and storage units are some of the easiest things you can do. There are even ready-to-assemble units you can add to the piece you are making, unless you are a purist who will only work with proper joinery. You can add plywood drawers with runners or wire drawers, etc to help you along. Visit a built-in wardrobe shop, kitchen shop or a big hardware shop to check out their range.

I was so broke when I made my wardrobes that for dividers I used plain old doors I had bought at a rural auction for $2 each, somewhat trimmed. I made the shelves from offcuts of Structafloor sheeting a carpenter had given me. Bargain! Some things in my house have been very cheap, others ruinously expensive. Oh well…

I recommend making built-ins for anyone with a hammer, a screwdriver and a drill. Hardware shops and lumberyards will cut everything to order—you don't even need a saw. They might charge a couple of dollars per cut, though, and you need to have very accurate measurements.

Carpentry—conventional roof

Rating:

This is one for the professionals I think. Go ahead and try if you like, but for me it's way too hard.

Carpentry—hanging doors and fitting locks

Rating:

Leave the doors in the house for a week before you hang them so they can adjust to your moisture levels. Hanging a door is quite fiddly; I have never done a door perfectly in my life. Fitting locks is also hard. You want your door to work really well so it isn't a source of irritation for years to come! It has to swing freely, without rattling or jamming.

I am not a perfectionist and I would only recommend hanging doors for those of you who are. Allow it to take you a day to fit a lockable door.

Carpentry—roof trusses

Rating:

You have two choices here. The easy way is to have the trusses delivered and just put them up. Depending on their span you will need some help here. I did a 4.5-metre (15-foot) span with one helper, an 8-metre (26-foot) span with two. Once you get the first truss up and tied, the rest is easy. You need lots of long rope with which to anchor the first trusses, and you might have to secure them to strategically placed cars, fence posts or whatever you have available. Trusses are fun and not very hard once you get the hang of putting them up. To learn the basics should take you about two hours. However, if

you have an issue with heights, don't even think about it. I recommend trusses to fearless agile people who like a fun challenge.

The other option is to make your own trusses. Your plans should specify what kind of truss you need; there are various designs for length of span and wind speed. If the plans are not specific, ask the engineer who drew them for more detail.

Trusses are quite easy to make. All you need is a circular saw and a large flat area like a concrete slab to build them on. The rest is just simple maths and plenty of hammering. The traditional methods of joinery are very beautiful for exposed trusses (I have never done this but I probably will sooner or later), but the easiest way of joining the trusses is with gang nails or nail plates. If you have a lot of trusses to do, but you're unsure of the maths and design, order one truss and then copy it.

Remember, the better the tools, the easier the job.

Your council will inspect the roof prior to covering.

Carpentry—second fix

Rating:

This includes all the finishing touches such as cornices, skirting boards, dados, chair rails and so on. Buy the best mitre you can. I used to have a wooden one; it was all I could afford. Regrettably, it wasn't very accurate after the first couple of cuts as the handsaw enlarges the mitre slot. These days I use a crosscut saw—a circular saw mounted on a swivelling plate for greater accuracy—but a metal hand mitre will do. A coping saw could also come in useful.

Second fix requires a lot of measuring, cutting, gluing and attaching. Double-check your measurements and do not attempt second fix unless you have reasonable tools (it will look really bad otherwise). In these days of mass-produced housing, this is a skill that is sadly fading away as few people will hire fine joiners any more. As a result, I recommend second fix carpentry

to anyone who is careful and accurate. You can make big savings by doing it yourself and it's a pleasing job that makes your rooms look really good.

Carpentry—wall framing

Rating:

Stud walls are often built on your slab floor, and then simply raised into position. You can certainly do this yourself, but read a book first; it is too involved to explain in detail here. The building plans will thoroughly cover your framework, so follow that. For speed, get a nail gun and an air compressor. However, you know how much it hurts when you hit your thumb with a hammer? Imagine the nail shooting out with the force of a gun! Be very careful. There are many unpleasant stories about nail guns. I hired a carpenter once who shot himself in the calf. He shared some expletives with me, prized the nail out, wrapped the leg up and kept working. The only other tools you'll need are a hammer, levelling equipment, stuff to measure with, and a circular saw.

I don't recommend this for anyone working alone, as you will constantly need two pairs of hands. But timber is very forgiving—if something isn't right it's easy to fix. Build a cubbyhouse or a bike shelter first, using the correct techniques, to find out if this job is for you.

Carpet laying

Rating:

The firms that sell you carpet will install it for such a competitive price, that it hardly seems worth the bother of doing it yourself. However, if you choose to, it's an easy job that you can master quite quickly. I'm not a big fan of carpet myself—I prefer rugs you can shake outside, instead of a carpet nailed down for years and years capturing dust underneath. I will admit, though, that carpets are nice and soft underfoot and do help to reduce noise.

Colour selection

Rating: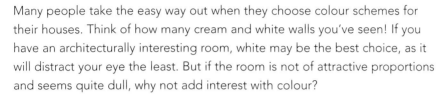

Many people take the easy way out when they choose colour schemes for their houses. Think of how many cream and white walls you've seen! If you have an architecturally interesting room, white may be the best choice, as it will distract your eye the least. But if the room is not of attractive proportions and seems quite dull, why not add interest with colour?

Not everyone is able to think of colour schemes that work well, so they stick with what's safe. However, painting your rooms in different colours is a cheap and easy way to direct the feel of the house. I have a lot of white in my home, I admit, but it goes so well with the strong blue of the woodwork and the red terracotta floor. My old house had a lustrous yellow-orange hallway and living room; a rich red room with a ceiling full of thunderous blue-grey sky; a white and green room; and a Queen Anne-style Chinoiserie room, with walls full of sanded-back gnarled trees, birds, flowers, butterflies and other insects. The orange I used in the hallway was a shade from my childhood that is forever burnt on my retina. It is the colour I saw when lying on hot granite cliffs after bathing in the fjord, all wrapped up in a yellow towel. The light filtering through my cocoon glowed yellow-orange. Just seeing that colour makes me recall the sting of salt on my skin and the splash of wet hair across my cheek.

Different people will respond differently to the same shade, so use your instincts. There is so much pleasure to be had from colour. Don't bother with the small paint pot samples: use clothes, towels, sheets, coloured paper or giftwrap, even a bunch of flowers, to help you find your perfect shade. Anything coloured will help you to imagine what the room could look like and you can then get the exact shade you want mixed in the paint store.

Colours are said to influence the way you feel. For example, some fast-food joints are decorated in bright red. This is believed to increase your hunger, but speed you up so that you don't want to linger. Perfect!

Here are some of the more common colour connotations:

- Purple—spiritual, regal

- Red—passionate, active, hungry, alert, warm

- Pink—calming (or nauseating if you ask me, although my bedroom was pink when I was 13 and I adored it)

- Orange and yellow—happiness, vitality, creativity, positive high energy

- Green—soothing, healing

- Blue—calming, inspiring, fresh and cool

- Brown—earthy, secure

- White—clean, pure, innocent

- Black—negative, death, depression, magic

Don't be concerned if you find you disagree with some of the associations given above. After all, surely not all greens are soothing? I don't think lime green would be particularly relaxing, as there is too much yellow in it, and I can also think of several greens that are plain repulsive. Nor can you say black is always depressing; I have a delicious little black cocktail dress that never depresses me! However, I guess large amounts of black could be seen as a negative element in your house.

Many intensive care units, maternity hospitals, etc are painted pink for its calming influence. Would pink prison cells have a calming effect on violent inmates? Some prisons have actually been experimenting with colour since the 1970s; our local one has cells painted pale blue, pale green and cream. Blue and green are both soothing colours.

Whatever colours you choose, make sure they have the right effect on you! Paint the bathroom fresh, the kids' rooms calm and creative, the kitchen joyous and your bedroom pure and soothing with a touch of inspiration.

Concreting

Rating: ↖ ↖ ↖

Concrete is cheap, strong and versatile. The old Romans invented it and we haven't stopped using it since.

Simple small concrete slabs and foundations supporting garden walls and suchlike are a good grounding for how to lay foundation slabs (if you really want to do them). Depending on how much you need, you can mix minute amounts by hand in a wheelbarrow, hire a concrete mixer, or order ready-mix in a truck. I've done all of the above, and the ready-mix is very stressful. You have to make sure you have plenty of people on site to run around with wheel-barrows and compact and level what comes out of the concrete pump if you are using one, as it will set faster than one person can manipulate it. Have a tarp ready where the truck can dispose of any leftovers until you decide where you want to put it. A truck with ready-mix represents excellent value for money, however, if you compare it to the cost of hiring a mixer, your time spent mixing the concrete and the chiropractor appointments afterwards.

If you need to change fresh concrete at all, do so as soon as possible, as it cures harder and harder each day.

Don't concrete when it rains. The drops will make the concrete too wet and damage the surface. You want water on the concrete, but not until it has set. As soon as the concrete has hardened a bit you need to cure it for maximum strength. This entails forcing the concrete to dry as slowly as possible. You can cover it with building plastic, paint it with a special membrane or water it several times a day. I hosed my slab down in the morning, then came home at lunch and repeated the exercise. I watered it again after work and in the evening too.

Though quite strong, concrete will crack easily and needs reinforcement. With concrete for paving, for instance, you can angle grind a sheet of steel mesh to place into the concrete. The concrete can certainly still crack, but the difference is that it will no longer move like continental shift. With foundations you use reinforcement ('reo') rod. This is a steel rod with little

raised ridges that stop it from moving once the concrete has set. Reo rod comes in different thicknesses and your plans will specify which is the suitable gauge for your needs and how many of these rods you must use.

Concrete surfaces can be finished in so many different ways: you can polish them, put colour through them, pepper them with glass chips and then grind them smooth, pebble them… The options are immensely varied, and more ways are being discovered all the time as people begin to realize concrete's potential. All you have to do is seal it. Play around, and pay attention to other people's floors. I've seen some gorgeous concrete floors and, while they might cost more initially, you don't have to pay for any floor covering afterwards!

Demolishing

Rating:

Depending on what you want pulled down, this can be a rewarding exercise but a potentially hazardous one too. If you are demolishing a whole house, get the professionals in. If there is a lot of salvageable building material it will reduce the cost.

However, if it is just a small lean-to, for instance, you can easily do it. Hire a skip, then start with the roof and work your way down. If you take it apart gently, you will be able to sell a lot of it afterwards or use it yourself. Wear a mask as dust protection, and make sure there is no asbestos involved. Have a garden hose ready. If big dust clouds rise, spray a fine mist to settle them.

If your demolishing is on a smaller scale—to make a hole in brickwork for doorways, etc—start gently chipping the mortar out from around one brick. Once the first one is gone, the rest will ease out. Keep a jack handy to support the wall in case too many stones or bricks want to follow. Make sure that the wall isn't load bearing. You can do that by looking in the roof space. If nothing rests on the wall, it is not load bearing and it's therefore safe to proceed.

Earthmoving

Rating: 🔨 🔨 🔨 🔨 🔨

Can you operate a bobcat? I can't. Like most people, I have to pay for my earthmoving. If you are truly keen, there is nothing to stop you from learning how to do it, but I certainly wouldn't recommend it unless you are planning to make it your next career.

If you are laying concrete foundations, make the earthmovers scrape the topsoil away before they start working on slab excavations. You can keep the soil in a pile until you have finished construction, and then spread it out when you are ready to start landscaping.

While the professionals are scraping at the ground, you also have an excellent opportunity to check your levels and get them corrected straight away. I have twice made the expensive mistake of trusting the operators to do this, but I can tell you that they won't do it of their own accord. It's not part of their standard brief. Afterwards it is much harder to correct your levels, as there are pipes in the ground that cannot be driven over, or perhaps a part of your house is in the way, preventing access for machinery. I have had to do hard labour digging with a pick and shovel to get the levels down. In the end I have simply had to opt for raised garden beds in order to avoid going deeper. As any paving surrounding the house will raise the levels, do you need to excavate further now? Where will any water drain to? If you live in an area of heavy downpours, you must be sure the rain will drain away fast so it doesn't build up. Work out these details *now*.

You can check your levels with poles hammered in the ground, some stringline and a spirit level. Beware of using stringline with a little spirit level attached; it is misleading, as the string will sag over distances and weigh the spirit level down. A very accurate way of checking your levels (*real* builders use lasers—these can be hired) is with a piece of clear hose open at both ends, available from the hardware. To do this, you need two people. First fill the hose with water, making sure there is no trapped air. One person will hold the level of water against the post in the ground; the other carefully and slowly

waits for the water to settle at the other end and marks the level. You will need to use this technique when you check levels over distance in brickwork, too. It doesn't look as sophisticated as the laser, but works just as well!

When you hire earthmovers (as with any trade, really), make it extremely clear what you want. They don't usually mind read. Draw a profile of the site, stating how much you want the ground to slope and where. This is a tricky undertaking that requires some thought, but it will pay off later.

Electricity

Rating: ⚒ ⚒ ⚒ ⚒ ⚒

Electricians aren't cheap, but you can't do the wiring yourself. It is illegal and potentially deadly. You will only be able to act as a lackey for a qualified electrician. However, running trenches in walls or the ground for your sparkie can still save you a lot of money, as these are the time-consuming tasks that make the cost add up.

Foundations—concrete slab

Rating: ⚒ ⚒ ⚒ ⚒ ⚒

I believe foundations require skilled, qualified people, and must be properly designed by engineers. My advice is to attempt them only if you are supervised by a suitably qualified person.

Having said that, I also recommend you don't trust that the professional will do a good job. You must have enough knowledge to inspect the finished job properly as, while the council will inspect prior to pouring, you must inspect before you pay for it.

I had a concreter in town do my slab extension. I assumed he knew what he was doing. Well, he might have been good with concrete but he couldn't read plans. The slab was not entirely square, but this I only noticed when the carpenters complained. What I *did* notice was a strange recess placed in the middle of the floor in what was going to become the bathroom. I looked at

the plan, and it was the skylight. My concreter had *recessed the skylight* instead of the shower area! Embarrassed, he cut out the shower recess, as the concrete was still green, and filled in the 'skylight' with extra concrete. But if I hadn't noticed his mistake, I would have had a pretty strange bathroom. The slab also sloped very unevenly. (The easiest way to check how the slope falls is by watering the slab, turning it into a giant spirit level.) My present slab is incredibly even; there are some ups and downs, but for such a big floor it's outstanding.

Gas fitting

Rating:

Don't touch it. This is a job for licensed people only. Working with gas is the stuff of nightmares, as you can die or blow the house up. There are legal restrictions that have to be obeyed as well.

Glazing

Rating:

For an easy way to glaze, that will also save you some money, get the glaziers to come and pin the glass in place. Then you can fiddle around with putty or beading afterwards.

Gyprock

Rating:

This is simple, light work that gives fast results. It's very rewarding and I recommend it to anyone. The difference between a professional Gyprocker and me is in the finish, as I just don't care enough to make it 'perfect'. Other people will be very neat and thorough.

There is a set of products that you have to use, and if you follow the instructions it isn't hard at all. I have a rough peasant house, with some Gyprock on the second floor. I didn't want a smooth finish, as that would have

looked incongruous, so I trowelled a rough plaster finish straight over the Gyprock. I didn't have to bother with any sanding and smoothing that way, and it looks much more suitable. My son and I did the Gyprocking together, as it helps to have someone lift the sheets with you. Relatively speaking, they weigh the same as meringue but are large and unwieldy. However, you can cut them easily with a knife, which is such a delightful change after all the dangerous and dusty machinery cutting that's required to build a house.

Insulation

Rating:

No worries here—just buy a product that's safe to handle. Some insulations are so safe they don't even require dust masks to be worn. Get those! Then prepare to be hot and uncomfortable for a while as you struggle on in the roof cavity. It's a simple job, however, and I recommend it for anyone who has an icy beer in the fridge for when they've finished. Beer and insulation go well together…

Kitchens

Rating:

The price you pay to have a kitchen made is over-inflated. Most of them aren't that finely crafted and they are often full of 'fake' stuff like laminates and chipboard. Go and look critically for yourself. These kitchens do not inspire you to part with lots of hard-earned cash.

However, planning and building your own kitchen can be great fun, and you get to develop your own ideas. It is *not hard*. All you'll need is a drill and a circular saw. Before you decide to go ahead, complete another simpler built-in project. If you can make a bookshelf, you can do the kitchen. The principles are the same, just with the added trickery of doors and drawers. If you hanker after things like lazy Susans, buy them readymade to incorporate into your design. The same goes for drawers—they can be bought as kits.

By doing it yourself, you can save *big* dollars—money that can be better spent on top quality appliances.

I recommend building a kitchen for anyone able to make a simple box structure, and brave enough to flout convention by not getting a standard one installed by someone else. I dare you!

Leadlight

Rating:

This is quite easy to do if you have a lot of bandages handy. I find leadlight brings magic to a room if well designed. You will need:

◆ glass

◆ an oil cutter

◆ a leadlight instruction book (I learnt from *Australian Leadlighting* by Paul Danaher and Dexter Johnson, published by Greenhouse in 1987)

◆ some lead, flux and solder

◆ a soldering iron

◆ a fine black marker with which to draw the design (it must be the same thickness as the core of your lead)

◆ some large sheets of paper for the design

◆ and a sheet of chipboard or similar with a right angle in thin timber nailed to one corner.

Practise your cuts on some clear broken glass—ask a glass supplier to give you his scraps—until you have stopped bleeding, and then make a small leadlight window as your first project. Don't cut your expensive coloured glass until you feel confident. The bigger the ripples and bubbles in the glass, the harder it will be to cut. Don't use that glass for tricky shapes. Once you've mastered the techniques, you probably won't stop

until you have done the whole house. Then you'll have to move so you can start again!

I have the loveliest views where I live and excessive amounts of leadlight would spoil them. However, my last house was full of leadlight and I bled copiously over all of it. These days I wrap a bit of masking tape on my most common places for cuts before I even start.

Bear in mind that lead is poisonous. Don't let children play with the scrap, and scrub your hands and nails before you eat, drink or touch the baby. Vacuum the area where you work regularly, as glass will sometimes shatter sending out fine sprays of glass shards. Don't set up your workspace in the kitchen for this reason! I used to have my front veranda set up as a leadlight space when my son Angus was little. On warm summer nights I would put on some insect repellent, turn on the outside light, and work away with my faithful dog by my side. Late-night passers-by would nod in greeting. It was lovely!

If you are crafty and/or artistic, and like fiddly bits, this is for you.

Light globes—changing of

Rating:

I hate changing anything and unashamedly prefer someone else to do it for me, but I *can* do it. Big cities could easily sustain a business that only changed globes for people: 'The 24-hour Globe Service—Any Globe, Any Time'. I can hear the phone pealing with incoming business already…

Change halogen ones while holding on to them with a tissue. Any direct skin contact will shorten the life of the globe. For all other globes, check you have the correct wattage. Stockpile a few and you will never be left in the dark again.

I once heard the comedian Judith Lucy say she had to apply her mascara by fridge light as all her other globes had blown. Well, it would certainly save on electricity…

Masonry—aerated concrete

Rating: ⌐ ⌐ ⌐

Otherwise known as Hebel blocks, aerated concrete is a very easy material to work with. It will cut with a handsaw, you can scrape off mistakes, and blocks just glue together. A child could do it! But, the dust it creates is very bad for you and you need to make sure you don't inhale it. So, all that handsawing and scraping is out of the question unless you wear protective gear and vacuum up all the dust afterwards.

I was initially tempted by this kind of brick because of its lightness. You are building with something so light it floats in water, like pumice stone. However, if your aerated concrete wall decides to crack, it has no flexibility and will crack the whole way very easily. As the mortar courses are very thin, you must ensure you start off straight with a level surface.

I recommend aerated concrete for builders with bad backs. Just wear a mask! It has also lately become very popular to carve sculptures from Hebel blocks, as the material is so easily scraped. You could make some lovely high relief panels for your walls.

Masonry—concrete blocks

Rating: ⌐ ⌐ ⌐

Concrete blocks are quick to lay as long as you choose the larger blocks. If you use the normal brick-sized ones, the same principles apply as for standard bricklaying.

Aim to get perfect corners, which is quite easy with the larger blocks, then you can flawlessly fill in your courses. Render over the whole thing and you have a beautiful wall. (Rendering also means you can get away with some imperfections in the construction.) My first building used these blocks: I built a 4.5 x 6-metre (15 x 20-foot) room in two weeks. The only drawback to using concrete blocks is their heavy weight. I would recommend it to anyone with good physique.

Masonry—exposed bricklaying

Rating: ⚒ ⚒ ⚒ ⚒

Laying ordinary bricks is very hard to get right, but as bricklayers are expensive, it's something worth trying yourself. A beginner's bricklaying can look messy and wobbly, and is also very slow. If you're planning double brick you'll be at it for a while. I don't recommend bricklaying to anyone who hasn't practised a bit first and who isn't a thorough person. Perhaps start with a brick dog kennel to build up your skill. My bricklaying looks very amateurish, but I might have another go later...

Masonry—mud bricks

Rating: ⚒ ⚒ ⚒

You can learn to lay these in a day. Mud bricks are pleasant to work with and forgiving if you make mistakes. Your hands also escape constant exposure to mortar as these bricks are laid with mud. Did you know that 20 per cent of houses in southern France are made with mud bricks? In Australia they can sometimes be seen as a bit alternative, but I'd call 20 per cent mainstream.

Mud bricks can be bought ready-made, or you can make them yourself if you have loads of time and the right soil. (There are tests you can perform on the soil to ascertain suitability.) It helps to have big machinery to make them with. I wouldn't have the time or back strength to go to all that trouble myself. What if the bricks I made were of poor quality? Too much clay means they'll contract and expand with the weather; not enough clay is bad too!

Masonry—repairing cracks

Rating: ⚒

If you have cracks in your brickwork, you have to work out what's causing them. If your wall has a crack big enough to put your fist through, your house needs stabilizing first. Perhaps it needs new stumps; perhaps foundations have worn away or were never there in the first place; or

perhaps you need huge steel rods piercing the building, holding it together. If the repairs are this big, you need to do the structural stuff before re-pointing the cracks. You can work out if a crack is stable by gluing a piece of glass over it. If the glass breaks, the crack's not stable. If your crack follows the pointing of the mortar it isn't so bad, but if the whole wall is cut in the middle of the bricks you have a structural fault.

To repair a crack in the mortar, you'll need to rake out the old mortar to a depth of 12 millimetres (½ inch) or so, then brush out all the loose crumbs. Wet the channel to prevent water being absorbed from the mortar too quickly, and then fill the channel with fresh mortar.

Ordering the right amount of materials

Rating:

With some basic maths formulae and accurate measuring you can easily calculate the amount of materials you'll need.

(a) The area of a rectangle = height x width.
This is used to calculate the area of walls, ceilings, floors, etc. If there are doors and windows to take into account, calculate the area of each door and window and then subtract the answer from the total rectangle.

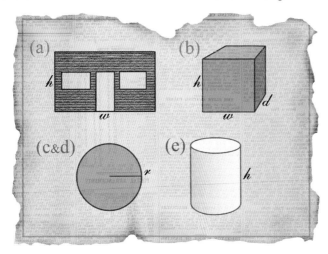

(b) The volume (contents) of a cube = height x width x depth.

(c) The area of a circle = πr2.
This means you will calculate 3.14 x the radius x the radius.

(d) The circumference of a circle = 2πr.
This means you will calculate 2 x 3.14 x the radius.

(e) The volume (contents) of a cylinder = πr2h.
This means you need to work out the area of the circle, then multiply it by the cylinder's height.

Outdoor drainage

Rating:

This is easily the most unpleasant job I've ever done. I needed to dig a trench that ended up sloping so steeply that I was standing in a trench up to my waist, digging in rock-studded clay with a jackhammer. Because I was using expensive hired equipment it wasn't something I could do a bit of and return to later—I had to do it in a couple of days so I could return the jackhammer. My tears of exhaustion mixed with the clay smeared on my face. I felt physically and mentally defeated! Elation followed, though…

For drainage you will sometimes need to bury pipes that can transport water away from your site. This means that you'll have to spend more time covering up what it took you so long to dig in the first place! It's a big job you can't even *see* in the end. Each job is different. Some are easy enough that you can use a special trench digger, but if accessibility is a problem, you might have to use a jackhammer like I did.

Painting

Rating:

Most people profess to be able to wield a brush and I recommend painting to almost anyone with at least one arm. Professional painters have been

taught techniques that give a better quality finish, however. Here are a few of their helpful tricks:

- Don't paint straight from the big can; pour some paint into a smaller container and replace the lid on the big one.

- Don't immerse the brush in the paint; only dip the first couple of centimetres at the most.

- Never scrape off excess paint against the rim of the container, this bad habit will create lumpy bits that will dry and fall into the paint. Press the brush against the inside of the can instead.

- Work fast enough to keep a wet edge.

- Use less paint and do more painting. Thorough brushwork will yield superior results.

- 'Spread the middle and starve the edge' is an old painter's adage that means you should finish all corners with a nearly dry brush. This will prevent the paint chipping and flaking as the edge gets knocked.

- Buy the correct paint, know when to undercoat, prepare surfaces properly, and paint in good light.

After you have sanded and cleaned your surface in preparation for painting, small bits of dust will remain. Make a 'tack-rag' to wipe the surface. Take a clean soft cloth, wring some turps through it, pour on a dash of varnish and work it through. You have now created a really sticky rag that will pick up every last bit of lint and dust! When you have temporarily finished with your tack-rag, put it in a lidded container so that it remains moist.

What happens if you hate the tint you end up with? After all, it can be difficult to know how the small colour sample will look on a larger scale. Fortunately, I like the colour-washed look and it's a great way to improve any colours you're not happy with. Make glazes and wipe over the walls with them. Have fun!

Here are a couple of recipes to get you started:

TRANSPARENT OIL GLAZE

1 part boiled linseed oil

1 part pure turpentine

Drier (How much you'll need depends on the kind. Some only require a teaspoon! This is optional; if the hardware store doesn't stock any, go to an art supply shop.)

A little whiting or Unimin (This is also optional. Add roughly one tablespoon per litre or ½ tablespoon per pint to give body.)

Mix all the above ingredients in a suitable container. Your glaze is now ready for use!

When you have made the glaze, you'll need to tint it. To do this, dissolve a squeeze of artist's oils (you won't need much) in some turps first, and then stir into the glaze. Take care to mix it well to avoid lumps of pure paint. Record how much you added in case you need to make another batch later. Experiment with a small section of wall and wipe it off again with a rag with some turps on it if it isn't yet right. Make sure you get lots of air whilst glazing or you'll pass out from all the turps!

Oil glazes take a long time to dry because of all the linseed. This is great if you need time to manipulate or distress the surface. They are also hard-wearing and have a luminous sheen.

WASH

1 small tube Gouache or acrylic paint from an art supply shop

1 litre (2 pints) water

Some regular water-based interior paint (Add a spoonful or three, depending on your desired effect.)

This is just one recipe for a wash; there are several methods. You could also simply dilute regular paint with plenty of water. If you require a thicker wash,

for distressing effects such as ragging, use one part paint to three parts water. However, don't apply a water-based wash over oil-based paint, as it won't stick.

The most important thing to remember when applying a water-based wash is to clean the walls properly, as the wash won't stick to any greasy spots. Use sugar soap, especially around light switches and doorframes where there's been a lot of greasy fumbling. Washes dry very quickly especially in hot weather, so you might find yourself struggling to keep a wet edge. If this happens, add a dash of glycerine.

Painting—decorative finishes

Rating:

The painted decorative tradition has a great history. Itinerant painters would travel the Swedish countryside, painting fake marble and exotic wood grain amongst other interesting finishes on people's furnishings and walls. The irony was that some of them had never even seen real marble, and were improvizing how they thought it would look. Their employers might never have left the region their whole life and so would believe that their painter's 'inspiration' was perfectly correct! Some itinerant painters specialized in floral motifs, and livened up the pine-darkened interiors of northern Scandinavia with hearty blooming roses on everything, from churches to potty cupboards.

Distressed finishes like ragging and stippling had an Australian revival quite recently. Special rollers and paint tins were developed to bring paint finishes to 'Every Man and his Cottage'. However, unskilled people have been doing these finishes for centuries without the help of special equipment. You don't need all that stuff; you just need a creative mind, some tubes of artist's paint, and a good book with pictures and recipes. The two recipes I've given above are enough to start you off: they will rag, wash, stipple, sponge, marble, etc.

My old house had several experiments on its walls. One of the best was an oil glaze that I tinted with a deep yellow, then washed onto pink walls and

finally dabbed with scrunched up plastic bags, After that it was left alone to softly blur on its own as the glaze slowly bled. Wonderful!

Paving

Rating:

The hardest thing about paving is levelling the ground correctly. If you don't manage to get the slope right, you will have water sitting in puddles forever afterwards. All water must run away from your foundations into proper drainage arrangements.

If you are building a new house, you will have details for your paving requirements in the engineer's report. Paving isn't hard, I'd even go so far as to say that it's fun. It's a job that gives quick results, really tidies up your site and stops the dirt from coming into the house. You need to compact some gravel and sand on the levelled site, and you will possibly need to hire a roller and a brick saw. If you have school-age children, check with their school if it will lend or hire out tools to parents.

Plastering

Rating:

If you are seeking to create a flat, even surface, plastering is very hard. If you like an aged look with imperfections in the surface, it's easy. This is a skilled trade, and for a good finish you'd better hire someone. I tried once, after repairing some salt damp. The wall was cured and only needed some nice flush plaster to blend in with the rest. I made such a bad job of it, it looked like the damp was still eating away at the wall. Potential buyers all commented on 'the damp'. It was frustrating to do all that work to the wall and end up with it looking worse than when I started!

Repairs to decorative plaster bits like cornices and arches are possible, but very hard to do well. Only do this if you are a meticulous kind of person or it will look bad.

Plumbing

Rating: ⚒ ⚒ ⚒ ⚒ ⚒

You are not allowed to do any plumbing that connects to town pipes. If you are on an independent system, like a septic system, you can. However, if you haven't done things properly and develop leaks under foundations because of it, you are in big trouble. My advice is to get a plumber who will work *with* you. You will dig the trenches he says, run the channels in the walls that he will mark out, be his dogsbody…but let him do the difficult (and qualified) work.

I have a great plumber, who knows I'm on a budget and lets me help. In my first house I had a weird arrangement, which entailed the plumber actually *paying* an hourly fee for digging to my husband and the lad next door, out of his quoted price! This was in the days of me not (yet) having learned to be assertive.

Plumbing—garden and roof

Rating: ⚒ ⚒ ⚒

I did my garden taps and pipes which was very satisfying. It felt like 'real' plumbing and wasn't very difficult. As long as you follow the instructions on all the products you use—primers, glues, thread tapes, etc—you shouldn't have any problems.

I also did the roof plumbing. You need two people who can cooperate in order to put up gutters. It can be complex since you have to be sure of adequate fall for the water to run off, and also have somewhere for it to go.

Pools

Rating: ⚒ ⚒ ⚒ ⚒ ⚒

When the heat descends there is no lovelier thing than to get truly wet without having to tolerate the hundreds crowding your local pool. I'd love

to live by the seaside, but since the sea is over an hour away, I thought a pool would do the job. However, while your own pool is a lovely indulgence, you have to think about several things. What will the running costs be? What kind of system will you use: salt chlorination, ordinary chlorine, ozone, bromine, etc? How much power do the pumps need? They'll need to run hour after hour and the cost of electricity is going up.

Size is another issue. I decided on a small one, as I find fencing so ugly that I wanted to enclose my pool completely in a room in order to avoid the fence requirements and still comply with safety regulations. Only a small pool would fit inside my planned room! A smaller pool would also require fewer chemicals, less cleaning, less water, etc; yet I'd still be able to swim, as I'd install swim jets. (If you want to swim on the spot but don't have any swim jets, you can achieve much the same effect by wearing a safety harness attached to something solid, like the pool fence.) I also wanted to tile the entire pool, and it would have been too expensive for me if it was any bigger.

It took a long time between getting the concrete poured for my pool to actually filling it with water. The company I had the initial contract with no longer existed when I needed them again, four years later. The owner had retired and sold the business. Luckily, I found him and he kindly agreed to complete the job anyway.

Words can not describe how happy I was to finally have water in it, but after a couple of days I realized to my utter dismay that the water was going down at an alarming rate. Hmm… I had paid for a completed job, and the leak warranty was only for the first year, but that first year the pool was dry. At this point I was very worried, and regretted the whole stupid idea of having a pool in the first place. But all's well that ends well. The retired owner fastidiously returned several times, until he found the reason for the leak and fixed it.

My verdict is to get the tradespeople in for things that involve water underground. It's difficult and costly to rectify them if things go wrong. You can always finish the job off yourself with paving, tiling, landscaping, fencing, heating, etc.

Rainwater tanks—preparing and plumbing them in

Rating:

In Sweden there is so much water, hardly anyone bothers to collect it. The sky keeps delivering more than you want and it can be heavily laced with pollutants anyway. Whenever I have Swedes visiting me they are so afraid to drink my rainwater they buy bottled water in the shop.

Here in Australia the water situation is a little different. In the countryside most people have tanks, and a lot of people are solely dependent on their ability to collect and conserve whatever water falls on their roof. I have no other source of water here, and it has to be enough. If you need or want tanks, decide where you want them to go at the planning stage of your project. They are not the prettiest structures but you can incorporate them into your design so that no windows look directly at them, for instance. You can also make use of climbers and other structures to conceal them. One of my 45,000-litre (10,000-gallon) tanks (I have two) is cornered by the carport, a Gothic woodshed, and a jasmine-covered walkway. You hardly pay any attention to it. Of course, you can also put your water tanks underground. I would have preferred this option but it was too expensive for me.

I love the idea of providing something for myself and collecting water requires no real effort. Water will be a bigger issue in years to come; water restrictions are common already. Water is the stuff of life. Collect it. The way things are going in Australia it won't be long before having adequate tanks will be a common building requirement. More tank shapes and designs are already cropping up. Perhaps one day, chunky veranda posts will be filled with water. Perhaps the average suburban boundary might be defined by a thick water-filled fence—just imagine the sound barrier it would provide! Perhaps the area under your house, if you are on a pier foundation, will be able to house an enormous tank.

In order to work out the capacity of your roof, you need to calculate your roof area and then find out your local rainfall.

1 millimetre of rain falling on 1 square metre = 1 litre

So, if you get 60 millimetres of rain, and your roof covers 200 square metres, you will put 12,000 litres in the tank.

For those of you more used to imperial measurements, the corresponding formula is:

1 inch of rain falling on 1 square foot = 4.153 pints (or roughly 4 pints for ease of calculation)

So, 5 inches of rain falling on a 2000-square foot roof will put 5190 gallons in the tank.

Work out how much you need to store. If you receive regular rainfall in your region, you will need to keep less in the tank. If you have three months that are dry, obviously you'll need more. My tanks just manage to keep the pool full, water the garden, keep the various inhabitants of the house clean and watered, and fill the stock trough.

If you choose a galvanized tank, you will have to build a tank stand. You can also choose plastic or fibreglass ones; these sit straight on levelled ground that's been covered with a good layer of sand to keep sharp bits away from the tank floor. Concrete underground tanks require a lot of spadework and I suggest you get a professional to come and dig for you. If you are going to operate a pump from you tank and plumb it into the house it's best to get a plumber to do it.

I have two constant pressure pumps on my tanks. One day, my goat Poddy had been tethered to the washing line in order to eat the weeds around there. He stretched himself all the way over to a garden tap, wound his chain around that, and panicked. Subsequently, he broke the tap, and the pump got a workout as the pressure sure proved to be constant. I managed to repair the damage, but with substantial loss of water.

The lesson here is: don't keep goats. There are a million reasons why you shouldn't, and about three as to why you should.

Roofing—metal

Rating:

The professional roofers will zap in and roof your house in a day or two. Absolute bliss!

For you, it will be an arduous task and a dangerous one, too. You will need to order your sheets and guttering to size. Then you will put up the gutters, with a suitable fall towards where the drainpipes will go. This is very tricky and requires two people. After the gutters are up, it should be plain sailing as long as the roof is square. You'll lay the sheets on the roof, ensuring they overlap in such a way that the prevailing winds can't rip into them. Before putting on the iron you should cover the roof with lapped sheets of sisalation, which is a reflective foil sheet. This important product acts as a vapour barrier and will shed moisture caused by condensation. It also reflects heat, keeping it where you want it.

Remember to screw into the ridges of the sheets, not the flat valley bits, as that will create leaks. The drill will try to slip and carry on. This is a tricky job, but you will get better at it. To avoid serious injury, never do roofing in any kind of wind or if the metal is the tiniest bit moist. A patch of water on a roof is as slippery as an oil spill and you don't want to fall to your death. A flying sheet is able to decapitate you. I have done some smaller sections of my roof and really enjoyed it, but had professionals in for the major bits. Good roofers are as agile as monkeys, and as fast and efficient as my dog on a ratting mission. I love them.

I recommend roofing for brave people without vertigo who can work well together, as anything but the smallest of jobs are not for people working solo.

Rendering

Rating:

Plain or ugly walls are easily transformed with a bit of rendering. It creates a Mediterranean look, especially if you put some coloured oxide in the render.

The steps for rendering are as follows:

1   Mix render in a wheelbarrow using plasterer's sand, sharp or brickie sand, a light coloured cement, and some oxide (if you want). The proportions of sand and cement are printed on the bags. If you are only doing a very thin one-coat render you can skip the plasterer's sand and just use brickie sand.

2   Wet the wall thoroughly with a hose. Do it at a time of day when the wall is shaded, as you don't want it to dry too quickly. Render the wall from the top down or the render will fall off. Work your way down and across. Hold a flat bit of wood full of render in one hand at right angles to the wall and scrape upwards with the other hand holding a metal rectangular trowel. When any loose bits of render slide off the metal trowel (and they will), they will only land on your wooden 'board' so it won't matter.

3   When the render starts to dry you need to rub it with something. Sponges are good but break apart too easily, so I suggest you use an old cloth. Dip it in water, wring it out and rub. This gives a nice sandy finish. If you want a glassy smooth surface, glide a wet steel float (a rectangular trowel) over it.

If you are rendering things that aren't absorbent brick structures, you will have to attach sheets of Weldmesh to your wall first. This gives the render something to bite on to.

4   (Optional) If you want a thicker render you need to do two coats, in which case you'll need to scratch the surface of the first coat in order to give the second coat a 'key' to bond with. You will replace step 3 with step 4 if you're going to do that, before repeating step 2 and finishing with step 3.

5   Gently sprinkle more water on it. By preventing the render from drying out quickly you 'cure' it, giving it strength.

That's basically it. It *really* helps if you have someone to help you; otherwise you end up with marks on the wall where the render has dried too much before you had time to continue. I have a rendered besser block

building that clearly illustrates this. I was in full panic mode as whenever I ran out of render and had to go and mix more, the render already on the wall would set.

I love surfaces treated this way as it can transform any masonry wall you don't agree with. If the idea of potentially stuffing up your house scares you, why not build a concrete block garden bench and render that first as an experiment?

To change the colour of any render, old or new, try this cement wash recipe. It will give a softly colour-washed Mediterranean look.

TRULY EXCELLENT CEMENT WASH

1 cup light cement

1 good spoonful of coloured oxide (more if you want a stronger colour)

water

Mix the light cement and oxide together with enough water to form a sloshy, milk-like consistency. Brush onto your rendered wall.

The result is simply stunning and very low budget. The wash doesn't flake or chip like paint does, and it costs only a fraction of the amount. The walls don't look painted, as the wash soaks in! I adore this style and all the effects you can create: deep red, vibrant sunny yellow, soft green…

Salt or rising damp

Rating:

Rising damp makes plaster go 'drummy' and has a pockmarked and flaky look. ('Drummy' is used to describe plaster that is not bonded to the surface beneath and which emits a noise like a drum when tapped.) If you have an old house, there is a good chance you have damp in it. They didn't build with damp barriers then, and had not yet invented any chemical additives.

Simply plastering over your damp patch will never work, as the damp just gets forced higher up when you cover the wall with a hard plaster coating. The damp needs to find a way out through the wall. The only option is to remove the cause and repair the damage. There are some different products and techniques available, but a failsafe and traditional method involves demolishing sections of your walls. Rest assured that this sounds scarier than it actually is! I took a short course in salt damp removal; the method described here is very thorough and straightforward and, most importantly, works for even the worst cases.

You need the following:

- a car jack

- a hammer

- a bolster for breaking bricks

- a cold chisel (a small pointy metal thing to prize the bricks out with)

- mortar mix

- coloured oxide to match (if your existing mortar is coloured)

- Expandite or similar

- liquid dampcourse

- black plastic dampcourse

- enough bricks to rebuild the wall again.

First, take the hammer and the cold chisel and chip away at the wall, starting at one end of your problem. If the salt damp goes right around the house, start wherever you feel like! Chipping away like this will feel weird if you've never demolished anything before—it's your precious house that you're pulling apart! Keep working away; you will end up with a hole in the wall. Don't make this hole too big, as the wall will collapse from the top if you do. This is why you keep the car jack handy. Get ready to prop the wall up if it starts to rumble. This is also not as scary as it sounds. Trust me! I was happily

working away on my wall when it felt like it was about to actually crack and come down. Panic-stricken, I ran inside and phoned my mentor who only then shared the car-jack trick with me. I will never again attempt salt-damp removal without a jack at hand.

When you have made enough room to start re-laying bricks, mix your mortar with liquid dampcourse, not water. This is expensive but you're not doing all this work to have the damp come back again. Put some mortar on the ground to level it, roll the plastic dampcourse onto the mortar and brick up the wall. You want the dampcourse to stick out, so the damp can't bridge it. When you reach the top of your hole-in-the-wall you will have a problem. Mortar shrinks as it dries, so you will need to use Expandite or a similar non-shrinking cement in the top layer, then wedge the wall tight with slate slivers or other hard, thin things.

Continue to move along the wall, demolishing and rebuilding at the same rate, until you have fixed the entire problem. When you have finished, you will have eliminated one of the major problems of old houses and you will feel terrific, even though your house (and you) now look an absolute mess. Don't worry, it will get better from here on. Now you are ready to render and plaster.

Sheds

Rating:

The trend in Australia seems to be that people spend a fortune on the house, and then erect a cheap prefabricated steel shed with minimum roof pitch prominently in the garden. I can hardly believe I'm saying this, but I once did the same. It was just a small toolshed, and I thought that if I bought lattice panels and trained climbers to grow over the whole thing it would look fine. But it was still an ugly building no matter how many climbers I put on it. If you start with a nice-looking construction, and then run the climbers over it, you end up with a charming building peeking through the greenery instead of an ugly one never quite successfully hidden.

Would you like an attractive tiny building in the garden? A woodshed, cubbyhouse, potting shed, storage shed or home office? Many councils will let you build a structure of a maximum floor area of 10 square metres (100 square feet) without building permission. No wall can be longer than 3 metres (10 feet) or higher than 2.4 metres (8 feet). This is an absolutely ideal starting point and confidence booster for you. You can apply all the same processes to your tiny building as you would to a full-size house. It is something you can achieve within a short time and it will make you feel fantastic. I built a 4 square metre (40 square foot) garden building near my planned house. It's in a lovely setting and provided my son with somewhere to go that wasn't a construction site as well as giving me more skills. It was his Christmas present when he was five, and we led him blindfolded to the two-storey cubby. These days, he is too old for cubbies and the goat has moved in; he seems pretty happy with the arrangement, enjoying the leadlight windows in his mock Tudor residence, surrounded by a low rock retaining wall and the old almond trees.

At the moment I'm making a really tiny toolshed in rendered besser block. I have planted flowers on the roof; if the roof eventually breaks down from the moisture I'll just do it again. I doubt that it will, though, as I laid some really substantial steel girders from a salvage yard on top of the walls, and then put down all my roofing scrap and old bits found on the land when we bought it. It was a nice clean-up! Over that I laid down some plastic, and 10 to 15 centimetres (4 to 6 inches) of soil. Then I planted gazanias over the whole thing, as they can withstand almost any conditions, even sparse soil in the baking sun without water—or so I hope! And there you have it, my version of a sod roof.

Soil—fixing it

Rating:

While improving the health of your soil isn't strictly speaking part of construction, it's something that you will certainly need to do once all the building's finished, so I've included it here. Your soil will be compacted

because of builders driving heavy machinery around. It could be full of bits of broken bricks, rubble and other rubbish. The topsoil could be ruined. Your soil is alive; it should be full of diverse living organisms and composting matter. It needs care. So, how can you give it a big invigorating boost?

Buying good quality new soil is one option. I did that once, as I had a house where the whole garden area had been covered in concrete for 50 years. I felt the soil needed replacing completely. It probably didn't, but I wasn't taking any chances before planting the garden. A bobcat man removed a truck full of the existing dirt, and then I hired a rotary hoe and mixed in tonnes of new loam. Was that necessary? I don't know, but the garden sure grew well. If you have a small garden area, this is a viable option, but you will possibly need to remove soil first or the ground level could rise too much. Pay attention to ensuring there are sufficient slopes for storm water drainage. For a larger garden, bringing in new soil may be prohibitively expensive. Simply covering the ground with a thin blanket of good soil won't do much good anyway, as it will form a useless crust on the surface.

At my present house, I covered my dreadful compacted clay with what I affectionately call 'a poo sandwich'. The ground all around the house was appalling; tractors delivering pallets of bricks and huge turning semitrailers had churned the clay into an almost impenetrable mass. I began the rescue process by sprinkling masses of gypsum on it, for its clay-breaking qualities. Then I put on a thick covering of soil that had been put to one side earlier by the earthmovers. It wasn't very good quality but it was the best I could do. Over that I put a layer of manure, anything I could find: sheep, cow, horse, whatever. I drove out to people's properties and bagged sheep manure from under the shearing sheds, mucked out stables, even drove around a cow pasture with a shovel.

I covered the manure with another thick layer of my existing soil sprinkled with some more gypsum and, as a final topping, a thick blanket of lawn clippings that my local lawn mowing man delivered. Instead of my heavy clay soil, I now had created a rich concoction that, after a few months, was teeming with earthworms busily aerating it and mixing it around. I am

against digging over the soil excessively; I feel it does little good and only creates more work for me. The worms will eventually do a much better job, as long as you keep them well fed, and you can buy extra worms too if you don't think you have enough. As worms love anything organic, all types of soil will benefit from adding organic matter. If you're not in a hurry to plant, you could grow a 'green manure' crop first. A mix of seeds that will quickly crop, this is more beneficial to the soil than plain weeds. Once the crop has grown, you simply dig it in and let it break down, gradually enriching the soil as it does so.

If you have a lot of weeds, simply soak newspaper in water and place layers of it on top of the stomped-down weeds. If the weeds have been slashed, they will puncture holes in the wet newspaper, so don't bother cutting them first. Then cover the newspaper with some kind of mulch. The weeds will die as the newspaper will block out the light. The worms will come and investigate the composting weeds, and improve your soil quality. I have done this whenever I have started a garden—even with waist-high weeds. The weed-reducing effect can last up to two or three years, depending on the type and depth of mulch you put on top. Newsprint has been rumoured to slow down growth as it leaches into the ground, but weeds can kill a young plant even faster. In my view it's the lesser of two evils.

Your food scraps can also help to enrich your soil, without attracting rats and mice. I bought a rodent- and fly-proof worm farm, which converts all scraps into rich compost. Basically, it's a series of black plastic crates stacked on top of each other. While the worms live in the bottom layers, you add to the top one, rotating the bins as they become full. I highly recommend this form of composting, as I find rodents absolutely horrible and they love feeding from ordinary compost bins.

Once your soil is ready, it's time to start planting. A cheap way to get a garden under way is to make use of cuttings. I went for walks around town, saw what plants appeared to be thriving without help and took cuttings of

them. In my area, daisies, rosemary, lavender, gazanias and geraniums are the star performers. Some plants propagate very easily—just break off a stem and stick it in the ground—but others require you to dust with a rooting medium before planting. For the cost of a few bags of potting soil and some rooting medium, I have established large areas of lavender, a 200-metre (650-foot) rosemary hedge, and embankments covered in bright-red geraniums and white daisies. I have never watered these plants, except for an inaugural soaking when I planted them.

You can have a no-water garden, even where it's very hot and dry, if you choose the plants carefully. Native plants are always a good choice. If you want a low-maintenance garden, be careful to plant things suited to your corner of the world. Nature doesn't get watered except by rain. You might have a local nature conservation society or catchment care group that will help you find suitable species.

Straw bale building

Rating:

Basically, this involves laying straw bales like enormous bricks tied together with steel rods, which you then cover with metal mesh and cement render. The walls go up fast. If you are interested, find a workshop where you can see the techniques being demonstrated. It seems easy enough to do as long as there are lots of you who can build quickly. Speed is of the essence, as you want your structure complete before any rain can fall. Choose the season! If this is your chosen material you will probably have to do it yourself as few builders specialize in it.

Tiling—floor

Rating:

Concrete floors that require drainage, like bathrooms and showers, usually require a render before you can tile. Otherwise the water might not make it to your drain but sit in puddles! Mix some mortar with a dash of cement

additive for increasing adhesion, paint some additive straight on the floor and then render away. Dampen concrete floors before you render them, to increase 'stickability' and lessen the risk of cracking. Make sure you get the slope right!

 I recommend you never use white grout. Use a light grey instead as white will quickly turn grey in patches anyway. It might as well be evenly grey from the start!

All concrete needs to be acid washed before you tile, in order to open concrete pores ready to accept the glue. Wear long sleeves, trousers and acid-proof gloves to protect you if you get splashed.

The preparation for tiling is much more difficult than the actual laying. Do a 'dry' laying first, checking where the cut edges will go. Draw a couple of lines to mark this on the floor. You can use a stringline dipped in chalk or even paint, and with the help of someone, stretch it on the ground. The layout could take a while, but take care to do this stage properly.

When you finally get to tile, lay all the tiles except for the edges and where pipes protrude. Wear kneepads to save your back and joints. Then, hire a cutter and do all the cuts in one swoop (your tile suppliers will cut any complicated circles). I did a complex combination of unglazed terracotta herringbone borders at my house, using an angle grinder for the cuts. In hindsight I would have been better off to hire a brick saw, as I burned out two cheap grinders and used up countless diamond blades. Grout up the joints the next day, and you're done.

Be aware that you will break tiles by walking on them unless they are embedded in the glue without any air gaps. That is why you should lay them with a slight 'slurping' twist.

As an aside, I will never again use glazed floor tiles near a back door that leads to a sandpit. No matter how much you try to prevent it, sand will get dragged in and dull the floor surface as it puts thousands of minute scratches in it.

I recommend floor tiling for anyone who can draw a straight line. For those of you who can't, I recommend mosaic which is much more free-form. You could, of course, combine the two. Have fun with it!

Tiling—wall

Rating:

This is supposed to be easier than floor tiles, but I think it depends on the surface you're working on. If everything is smooth and straight, it is obviously easier than if there are irritating knobbly bits that make the tiles wobble. Make sure you start straight! Nail a dead-straight timber batten to the wall, slightly lower than the height of one tile off the floor. Since floors are rarely even it isn't smart to start tiling directly from the floor. Tile upwards, using spacers so the tiles don't drag down. Plan the first course so you don't have awkward cuts at each end. Wall tiles are usually quite soft, and will cut with an inexpensive glass or tile cutter. Just score the glaze, place the score line over a pencil, and snap. It's a miracle!

When the wall is dry enough for the tiles not to drag down you can remove the batten and cut the bottom course of tiles. Grout the following day.

Wooden floors—laying

Rating:

Laying new timber floors is not hard; you just need a good saw and a hammer. Keep the boards inside for a few days before you lay them, so they can adjust to your indoor moisture levels. After that, lay them without further delay, as the boards will warp and twist if stored incorrectly for any length of time. Ensure you leave a small gap between the ends of the boards and the wall, in order to allow a little room for the boards to expand and contract in response to the changing seasons. Your skirting boards will cover this gap later. The new boards will only require a very light sand by hand prior to sealing them.

Angus and I laid our wooden floors together. We stained the underside of each board before flipping it over and nailing it into place, thereby doing the ground floor ceiling simultaneously!

Wooden floors—restoring

Rating:

Have you been blessed with some old wooden boards hidden beneath layers of newspaper and lino? Before you sand them back to remove the years of accumulated grime and damage, you'll have to countersink all the nails, as they will rip the sandpaper if they protrude. You can hire walk-behind sanding machines that look like lawnmowers, but they aren't as easy to use as you might think: they grip and put grooves in the floor if you're not careful. If you doubt your sanding skills, call in the professionals!

Any damaged sections of boards will need to be replaced. Take a sample piece of your floor around to demolition shops or stain new floorboards to match. Try this on an offcut first, as the varnish will alter the colour of the stain. You can also antique new sections to match the old floor. Dent new boards with a chain wrapped in cloth, apply some very dark stain and then sand it off. It will only remain in the deepest spots. If your existing floor has big black spots in all the nail holes, imitate that too. There are many ways to finish your newly restored floors, from liming and staining to glossy varnish. Explore the options.

8

If you have children on your site, which I recommend, you are definitely in for interesting times. I started renovating my first house when my son was four months old, which was a soft start as kids don't move around so much at that age. It was also good timing for me as I had a nice chunk of time off work. If you have a full- or even part-time job, when on earth are you going to find the time to work on the house without crossing over into your parenting times?

BUILDING WITH BABY

Babies are not very mobile so you can keep the power tools plugged in without fear. But how, when you have just spent an hour putting them to sleep, can you crank up the saw without waking them again? Some planning will be needed here, and I suggest you include the occasional late night so that you can get some uninterrupted quiet work done. Gentle noises like drills can be fine behind closed doors, but the sudden bang of a hammer might be too much. A consistent noise is better than a sudden one, too. I found I did the loud stuff when Angus was awake and saved plenty of quiet work for the sleep times. I actually thought he had a hearing impairment at one point, as he didn't react to the noise, but he was just used to it.

You will soon realize that it isn't easy to finish something when your most precious reason for renovating wakes up and demands your attention!

Compile lists of different things to do so that you can grab something without too much thought. Just pick a job from the list of 'Quiet Things to Do, Indoors' or 'Loud Things to Do, Outdoors', for example. This way you will have a hundred unfinished jobs but gradually they will all get done…don't worry!

However, if your baby can see you and talk to you, he or she is more likely to stay happy. My son would happily gurgle away in a bouncy chair or his pram just outside the open door of where I was working.

If he had been impossible to work with for a couple of days, I sometimes brewed myself some strong coffee and worked until dawn, while he slept. Then I would rest during the next couple of days, knowing the amount of work accomplished in an all-nighter far outweighed the amount done in the company of a grizzly baby. I haven't done that kind of thing for a long while, but parents of young children have to find whatever time they can.

If things get too hard, stop for a while. Does it really matter if that job doesn't get done this week? Maybe go to the beach for the day. Remind yourself of all your reasons for doing what you're doing. You are no good to anyone if you exhaust yourself mentally as well as physically.

On the plus side, babyhood is a great time to do up your kitchen since baby food requires little preparation. Catering is a breeze when your baby only requires milk and jar food at regular intervals! You'll also lose any surplus pregnancy weight, as you won't be able to cook. (See the section on 'Cooking without a kitchen' on page 159 for survival tips.)

IT'S TOUGHER WITH A TODDLER

This is a good time to memorize the Poisons Information Centre phone number—you could need it. You should also check that your ambulance cover is paid up. I needed the Poisons line once when my son, aged two, thought the delectable-looking bucket full of Gyprock goo was edible. It wasn't, but it wasn't poisonous either so he was all right. Now, *I* would never have left an open bucket of *anything* accessible to my little treasure, but the same doesn't necessarily apply to tradespeople. They're a different story altogether; after all, they're not being paid to baby-sit.

Do you have family or friends nearby who can look after the offspring for a couple of hours while you polish the floors? It's helpful if you have, as some jobs can't easily be stop-started. My family are all on the other side of the world, and I found it very hard at times. The most attractive item in the house to my son when very young appeared to be my shiny new bright-red circular saw. If I left it sitting on the floor, it would seemingly beg for his little podgy fingers to press the trigger! The best habit to form here is to immediately unplug every power tool after *every single* use. Then put everything away. I know this is inconvenient to say the least, but toddlers move with lightning speed, especially when you turn your back for a second.

My son and I also had adventures with roofing nails going down the toilet, and keys being dropped into open drains (remember that lovely plopping sound of things falling into water?). As if building wasn't challenging enough with just adults around!

Be very careful of regularly saying 'no' to your toddler when they want to help. By the time they are old enough for you to ask them for help they

might no longer want to. Instead, give them tasks that seem real to them. Nothing matters as long as they are happy and safe, and letting you get on with your work. My toddler took delight in helping me smash tiles with a hammer while I laid the tessellated veranda tiles. He approached his work very seriously and took pride in handling the same things I was handling, just in a different way. All kids want is to be a part of your day, and learn new things.

DEVELOPING YOUR PRESCHOOLER'S SKILLS

By the time your child has grown up a bit he or she will have a wonderful time being on site. They will enjoy making things with offcuts, paint, glue…anything that's going spare. Keep a box of non-toxic stuff they can use without asking. If your house is on a concrete slab, get some chunky pavement chalk. Right now, the kids can make floor art and you don't have to worry about the mess! Your house is, after all, a building site. Just remember that some material, like Permapine, is very poisonous. My son, to this day, when rummaging among offcuts will call out, 'Is this poisonous wood?' before using it. What a good boy!

It is a good investment to buy your child a junior set of tools that actually works. Don't waste your money on plastic stuff, as kids find imitation tools disappointing once they know what real ones are like. They can use steel retractable tape measures, small hammers, little screwdrivers and other functioning tools in relative safety. Put them all in a tiny tool belt or toolbox and your child will be more likely to leave your things alone, hopefully.

Building with a preschooler is an incentive to have a tidy site. When a tool goes missing you don't want to have to X-ray your offspring in order to find it. The first place I looked when things went missing was wherever my son was playing. If he'd had enough time to forget what he was doing an hour ago I would show him a similar tool as a memory jogger. Often he would find the tools but sometimes I was accusing him

unfairly. At times, I had no choice but to drive to the hardware shop to replace something I couldn't waste any more time looking for. There is a limit to human endurance! Some small tools were lost forever…

You might end up with an exceptionally creative, independent child. But there could be one drawback: getting them to tidy up afterwards. I almost always had to clean up after mine.

When the roof went up at our place there were some seriously good offcuts, enough for my son to build a small cubby in the paddock. It was a challenge for him that I encouraged, as he learnt about wind bracing, levelling flooring and just how stingy I could be when he asked for material I still needed for the house ('You get *all* the good bits, Mum!'). Then I tried to get him to demolish his disused, falling-down building a year later… He eventually did, but it took an entire year of asking.

YOUR PRIMARY SCHOOL HELPER

Let your primary school child be a real asset to your work. Give them some proper jobs, like being in charge of first aid. I had my son and his friends up to their armpits in a giant bin full of mud stirring it for me like a human Mixmaster. They did a great job! The added bonus was that I didn't have to do it. Keep aside some old clothes for them to wear when 'helping' so you can relax, then simply hose down your kids at the end of the day.

My son, aged ten, was absolutely invaluable when doing floors, ceilings and Gyprock. Sure, he may have grumbled a bit but I couldn't have done it without that second set of hands. Plus, he got paid! Angus also provided me with a steady supply of logical solutions to things, and scout knots for anything that needed tying. We spent some time puzzling out how to raise a half-built staircase and it was he who came up with the most workable solution. Consider your child an asset. When you are stuck, the fresh eyes of a child just might solve your problem. They have the ability to look at things in a new and unconventional way. Remember, too, that no one rises to low expectations.

If you build cavity walls, consider letting your children make a time capsule you can build into the cavity. They will amaze you with their creativity and provide someone with a fantastic surprise in years to come. Items to be included could be a greeting to the future finder; a list of the people who live in the house; how old they are and what they are like; and something with the date, like a newspaper page. Add your children's drawings or stories about what a day is like for them, coins, photographs of the house, how they feel about living there, what the neighbourhood is like, photographs of that…the list is endless. Let your children have most of the input. You can be sure that whatever they put in will be very exciting to someone in the future. Make sure nothing edible is included, then put it all in a vermin-proof container, like a screw-top metal canister or large glass jar. The closest I have come to finding a time capsule myself is when I repaired some salt damp in a house and found some old cardboard packaging stuck between the stones. That was exciting enough for me!

Remember that anything fume-producing or otherwise dangerous should only be done when children are not present.

If you include your children early on, even in small ways, the project will become a part of them too. Sometimes I feel twinges of guilt over the masses of time I have spent working on the house but I know Angus has gained from the experience as well.

You need to supervise your child when they have friends over, because the friends may not see the importance of the rules you have carefully instilled in your child. Remember the responsibility you have to them, and take extra care. Tell them they *will* be sent home if they disrespect the rules, and follow through on your threat if necessary. Nothing will put a dampener on your day more than having to explain to a child's parents why their darling is in intensive care. See the section on 'Public liability' on page 38 for further information.

Once, I found a young visitor actually rollerblading on top of my scaffolding, almost 3 metres (10 feet) up in the air. He had climbed the ladder *with skates*

on. My heart nearly stopped. If it is going to be too hard for you to supervise your child's friends, don't let them visit. Your house is a building site not a giant playground!

THE PROS AND CONS OF HIGH SCHOOL

If you are lucky enough to have a cooperative high schooler, you have a ready-made building partner. However, some high school kids are anything but cooperative and you may find it impossible to get any help from them. Perhaps you can encourage them to earn money by working for you, if you have any to spare! They can learn some useful skills and will feel a sense of project ownership. Even if they don't do all that much, when they show it off to their friends they will lay the pride on with a trowel. Anything you can do they can do too…perhaps better?

PREGNANT OWNER-BUILDERS

If you become pregnant after you have started, what can you do? You are no longer able to lift anything heavier than a cheese grater and must be extremely careful to avoid paint fumes or any other chemical fumes. The building work might have to grind to a halt, unless you are a hands-off type of builder. After all, there is nothing except nausea to stop you from organizing others! Just don't get carried away and try to do too much too quickly. Does the work really have to be finished by a certain date? If you tell the council your reason for wanting to extend your permit they are sure to be sympathetic. While the timing may be poor, a pregnancy only lasts nine months; then it's to the top of this chapter for you!

A final word

My son's verdict on growing up on building sites was, 'To me it feels completely normal, except compared with other families it's like living on the moon.' I think he survived the whole thing quite well…

9

STAYING ALIVE
and other hazards

IN WHICH WE LEARN TO DEAL WITH
VERMIN AND HOW TO WRAP UP
A SEVERED FINGER

Building sites present numerous hazards. Apart from the dangers posed by power tools and scaffolding, there are also spiders and snakes to be wary of. My collection of injuries is fortunately very small— perhaps this is because I'm sometimes a big chicken or perhaps just because I've had outrageous luck. I have, however, had some near misses. You are no good to anyone if you are injured! Building sites are dangerous places and you will need to take a lot of care. Professional tradespeople die on building sites all the time. Don't follow their example! Buy the right safety gear (and use it), keep your site tidy, and learn basic first aid.

SAFETY GEAR

Your safety gear is your first line of protection and includes earplugs, ear muffs, gloves, hard hats, sun hats, sun cream, kneepads, back braces, dust masks, respirators, covered work boots, sunglasses and safety glasses. While some items are self-explanatory, there are others that need to be looked at in more detail.

Gloves

There are gloves to suit every task! Grippy gloves are available for grippy jobs; leather gloves are good for protecting you against snakes, spiders and splinters; acid-proof ones will prevent chemical burns (and you will need to use acid if you plan to tile anything), etc, etc. There are even special gloves for carrying sheets of glass—particularly useful on a hot day as otherwise glass will start to slip through your hands. When working with cement you'll find your hands will dissolve and eventually become open festering wounds if you are gloveless for any period of time. Cement acts as a corrosive! Unfortunately, I like to work with bare hands as much as possible as I get a better 'feel'. I also have a theory that, while gloves wear out, hands repair themselves!

Hard hats

These are useful if you have people working overhead, as they might drop tools or similar hard objects. I worked alone on site, and so didn't need to protect my head from objects dropped by others, but I do use a hard hat whenever I am chainsawing. The moving chain can kick back straight up into your forehead if you are unlucky. I don't want to rely on luck when I saw…

Kneepads

When working low—tiling, for instance—kneepads are great. You don't want to crawl around with your knees unprotected, as this will give them that rough peasant callused-knee look. Once I used a toddler's nursery chair that

my bottom could wedge into tightly and simply hopped around on that. I wasn't embarrassed at all and it worked a treat, but now I have proper black kneepads. They have the added advantage of making me look like a Transformer (for those of you not in the know, this is a kind of robotic toy), which is fun and sexy. Buy a second pair and put them on your shoulders to complete the look!

Back braces

A back brace not only supports your back when doing heavy lifts, it also creates a firm corset effect that makes you look sensational! If I plan to carry heavy objects around for a while, I'll put my back brace on because it feels great. It can also help to keep your pants up, if you've lost weight from all your building work.

Dust masks and respirators

These work much better than simply pulling your jumper up over your mouth, but they're perhaps not as convenient. Disposable dust masks are sufficient for most things but I keep a proper respirator with a replaceable filter for *really* unpleasant jobs. The drawback with a respirator is that the tight rubber strip that holds it on your head rips your hair out. If you are going to use one often, perhaps visit a diving shop and get a special fabric cover for the strap to protect your hair.

Some dust is worse than others. Any demolition dust is dodgy, as you don't know its history and contents. The dust from fibrous sheet products such as Hardiflex or Villaboard, and powdered Hebel blocks is definitely not worth inhaling. I realized how scary this invisible enemy could be when I discovered termites in the old lean-to of my first house. The termite man treated the area, and then dabbed some arsenic onto the roof joists so no termites would bridge the area into the main house. I remember thinking at the time that the poison would all come raining down on us when we were demolishing. Old buildings are all potential toxic-dust hazards. Wear a good mask or respirator and if outdoors, use a fine spray from a garden

hose to settle any dust as quickly as possible. Wet fibres are harmless. Treat everything as poison and you'll be safe.

Covered work boots

Proper work boots are useful for preventing injuries to your toes. A guy I know likes to work in thongs but I just couldn't. That's so unsafe! I end up with a labourer's tan every summer as I wear traditional work boots with socks and shorts. Not very attractive, I know. I try to continuously roll my socks and shorts up and down in order not to have any sharp tan marks. I know I'm vain, but I just hate how much shorter your legs look when striped horizontally.

Safety harnesses

If you are working in an area far off the ground that has unsure footing, like roofs or my 7-metre (23-foot) dining-room ceiling for instance, you might feel happier if you are attached to a harness. I know I do. I strap myself in, and have a little swing to test if it can take my weight comfortably. The fear factor loses a lot of its power if you know you will stop short of the ground in the event of a fall. I had to do the last section of my ceiling without the harness, as there was no longer anywhere to attach it to. I was bathed in a cold sweat the whole time wondering what the point of building two storeys was if I would lose the use of my legs as a result. Assuming I even survived the fall onto hard concrete, of course.

When doing high and dangerous work, it is good to have two people on site. That way there is always someone who can call the ambulance if one of you needs it. Make sure you each know what to do in the event of an emergency.

HAZARDS

There is a lot you can do to make your building site as safe as possible, most of it just requires a little common sense. The following are some potential hazards you should look out for.

Chilblains

Now here's a hazard you might not have expected! Why devote a whole section to chilblains? Because I've got them and I don't want you to get them too. Exposure to the cold can damage capillaries and this damage can be *permanent*.

My hands would become cold and wet working outside on the building in the winter; they'd get so cold they ached. I then made the mistake of warming them up too quickly, by placing them under warm running water. The sudden heat aids capillary damage. What you end up with is fingers that itch, feel hot and swell up to an attractive red meaty appearance. They can turn blue and even develop hard-to-heal ulcerous wounds if you scratch them.

No one really knows exactly what causes chilblains, or how to make them better, but there are a lot of rough guesses. Call me naive and ignorant but I didn't know about them! Be comforted by the fact that not everyone exposed to cold will develop chilblains. Some people seem more sensitive to temperature changes. I have been told that the elderly, sedentary and anaemic are the most susceptible. Well, what does that say about me? I'm most certainly not elderly, and at the time I was very fit, spending hours each day running around with bricks in my hands. My fingers have been all right this past year but chilblains recur easily once you've had them. Take care and do what you can to avoid being one of the unlucky victims.

The following are some tips on how to prevent chilblains.

- Avoid long exposure to cold.
- Keep your whole body warm.
- Exercise to improve circulation (you will already be doing this if you build).
- Wear warm gloves.

I've also included some unscientific ideas on how to make them better, if you get them.

- Eat fresh ginger or drink ginger tea.

- Take bioflavonoid—apparently it can help maintain capillary strength.

- Take ginkgo biloba, available in health food shops—this can help support the distribution of blood supply to the fingers and toes.

- Don't scratch as you'll damage the skin (easier said than done—this is the itchiest thing I have ever felt).

- Don't apply direct heat.

- Apply calamine or witch hazel lotion. Someone once told me to mix glycerine with detergent and a little water, and rub it in. It seems to help! (And by the way, this recipe also makes great soap bubbles if you add more water.)

Electricity

Electricity is very dangerous stuff. Ensure your electrician puts in a circuit breaker. I shorted something once, there was a blue flash and everything went dark. Don't underestimate the power running through the little wires! Frequently check your extension leads and discard any that are damaged. Don't overload power boards and only use those with surge arresters. Don't work in the rain with power tools, if you have to run cords outside make sure the connections are kept dry.

Never use extension cords that are not fully uncoiled, and don't coil them up unless they have been unplugged first. Plugging them in generates electromagnetic flux (just trust me on this one) which leads to heating within the coil. This can melt insulation, as the wire in the coil shorts out.

Equipment condition

This sounds basic but is very important. I'll tell you why. If you are poor or mean, you might well try to force a bit more mileage from worn equipment. This is not a good idea!

My longest ladder was an old wooden one, and I was reluctant to throw it out, as it would mean buying another. I knew it was getting on a bit, but hoped it might see the building through… It didn't. I had ignored the warning signs of a worn ladder at my peril. My plumber laughed at it, my electrician wouldn't use it, but I did. So what happened? I was going down the ladder one fine day thinking how nice a coffee would be about now when a ladder rung snapped. As I fell onto the next rung, that snapped too! I held on to the sides of the ladder picking up splinters as I careered out of control to the floor. Not only did I end up having to buy a new ladder anyway, I also suffered some totally unnecessary cuts and bruises. I might as well have bought a new ladder when I saw how worn the old one was getting…

This warning also applies to power tools, hand tools, extension cords, hire equipment, and whatever else you can think of. If you see any damage, *stop* using the equipment. Fix it or buy new. Trying to save money by being unsafe is *stupid* and not something you should do.

As an aside, I have since cut my old ladder shorter, sanded it back and suspended it from my kitchen rafters in order to hang pots from. It's finally safe—unless the pots fall down!—and very attractive, too. I washed the blood off first…

Power tools

You will use a variety of power tools, without doubt. Wear the right protective gear and please, *tie up long hair*. Any loose clothes must be tucked away too. I once had my loose work shirt get sucked into the electric planer, and the planer moved its way towards my hip with great speed. When it became too full of shirt it stopped, but imagine if the shirt had been long hair!

Many power tools have a handy mechanism that locks the tool 'on' once you've pressed the trigger. However, the only way to stop the tool is to press the trigger again. This means that a tool can career around on its own without you holding it. Things like circular saws are likely to kick back in

some situations. Be prepared. Be careful every time, even when you feel confident. Experienced carpenters lose fingers, what makes you exempt? Care, care and more care. Read the safety instructions first. Don't rush a cut. Plan what you are going to do and know that you have a steady footing, that no cords are going to get cut and that your hands are out of the way.

Don't use power tools if you are tired or hungry. I become weak when I haven't eaten for a while.

Roofs

Do you have vertigo? If so, pay someone else to get on the roof. I sometimes use a harness for working on the roof, with an extra person on the ground. When doing the timberwork I nailed some wood across two trusses at a comfortable stepping distance to create a built-in 'ladder'. This is much safer than scaling the purlins placed 1 metre (3 feet) or so apart. Wear a carpenter's pouch so you can leave your hands free for climbing.

If you are putting on a tin roof, *never* do it in even the slightest wind, as the metal sheets become uncontrollable lethal weapons. This was hard for me, as I live on a hilltop and most days have a breeze. Wear clean dry non-slip sneakers; my site was so muddy I would change shoes at the foot of the ladder. If there is dew on the roof, wait. Only a bone-dry roof will offer grip.

Learn how to safely overlap planks. You don't want to step on the end of a plank, which then flips, sending you plummeting to the ground.

Scaffolding

I guarantee you will need to get higher than you can reach from the ground, unless you are building a basement. Sometimes a ladder will be enough, but if you are laying bricks for instance, you need scaffolding. You could hire it, but that will be expensive, as you will almost certainly be slower than a team of builders. They might need it for a few weeks only while you could take a year, maybe more.

I started with a good solid plank suspended across two piles of bricks, but this was very hard to move around and totally inadequate. (By the way, don't use any planking you're planning to use for the building later, as it will soon become ruined.) When my plank proved insufficient I was lucky enough to be able to borrow a painter's scaffold, which is like two A-frames with a plank between them.

That wasn't enough either, however, as my house is just too high. Now I'm the happy owner of two different sets of scaffolding: a painter's one for small, lower jobs, and a professional collapsible platform on wheels that can be moved around. I recommend that if your project is big and looks like it will take a while, buy something second hand instead of fiddling around with potentially dangerous improvised stuff. You can always sell it afterwards and you'll have the pleasure of working in safety for the duration. I haven't sold mine because I think it could come in handy some other time… Buy the best scaffolding you can find, as you'll get your money back afterwards. If you keep hiring you most certainly won't. Check the classifieds!

Vermin and other wildlife

When my little sleepover house was completed, I furnished it in readiness for weekends. Then I left it alone for a couple of weeks as I returned to town. The next time I came up, I soon realized mice had moved in. If you leave anything vacant for even short periods, vermin will come. And if you have rodents, you invite snakes to join them. Snakes have a well-developed sense of smell and can 'smell a rat' much faster then we can! I live in a paddock, which doesn't help. Every living thing in a field will congregate to a building site. Last summer I had a baby brown snake inside, twice. I don't have mice any more, but the snakes probably came for the good atmosphere… However, the suburbs are not immune to snakes and all the other nasties either, so how do you minimize the vermin?

My idea of rodent control was to get a cat, but my husband thought that would only replace one vermin with another. Instead, we bought a Jack Russell puppy and called him Felix the Alternative Cat. Felix had good

mousing skills and would rally to the cry 'Where's the mouse? Where's the mouse?' but sadly, he wasn't nocturnal. Whenever I woke to suspicious noises I would grab Felix, put him in the kitchen corner and egg him on. He would yawn, blink a couple of times and retreat back to bed, casting me a reproachful glance as he went. There are no substitutes for actual cats! These days I have one, and I no longer have a rodent problem. Between Felix and the cat, the problem is solved. I do have a slight problem with the issue of cat ownership, as cats do kill so many things just for pleasure, but mine is wonderful at patrolling the house perimeter for vermin. She also spots snakes in the summer, and alerts us to their presence. Lately she has given us some lovely gifts in the middle of the night: live mice brought into the bedroom! We now close the doors.

Keep your site clean, and as free of rubble as possible. (The council will complain if the site isn't tidy enough, and has the power to issue fines.) Wear gloves for protection, never leave food around to invite rodents, and be aware of the potential for snakes when you lift things like metal sheets. Wear boots. As you build, you will find spiders under every second brick you pick up; snakes hiding under the pallets; and mice, rats and wasps going forth and multiplying in any pile of assorted debris. The speed at which this can happen will alarm you.

I learnt to wear gloves when carrying bricks, and though I used to be so jumpy I would fling a brick away if I so much as spied the scurrying hairy legs of an errant wolf spider, I have now learnt to accept their presence with stoic calm. Shivers no longer run up and down my spine when I see a wolf spider or the locally prolific redback. I just brush them off (perhaps a few have been crushed!), and I have not been bitten yet.

FIRST AID

If you—despite all precautionary measures—injure yourself or others, a little first aid knowledge won't go astray. Hopefully you'll never need it, but I'll be surprised if you can get through an entire project unscathed. You never truly appreciate good health as much as you do when it's gone.

Keep emergency numbers readily available and visible. By the phone is a good place. If you are injured, you may be in such a flap that you don't remember them.

Think of ways to make your access to emergency help as quick and easy as possible. Perhaps your building site has no phone yet. Perhaps you have no mobile phone, or you're building in an area not yet blessed with mobile reception. You could be in trouble if there is no one to hear the scream as you hurt yourself. Initially I had no phone on site, no neighbours within cooee and no mobile. However, I made sure that my car was always facing down the drive towards the road when I was working, so I wouldn't have to do any tricky turns if I was bleeding to death or had snakebite. A small precaution, but sometimes every second counts! You could also always try to have someone on site with you on days when you know you're going to be doing something potentially dangerous.

Assemble a first aid kit to keep on the site and learn how to use it. As a minimum, I keep a handful of bandaids for small bleeds (though masking tape will do) and a roller bandage for big ones.

I have outlined a few simple first aid guidelines below, but they are no substitute for a proper first aid course.

Bites of all kinds

If you should happen to be bitten by something, keep still and don't panic. Try to see what it was that bit you, but don't try to kill it as it might bite you again. Do not wash any venom off your skin. Instead, apply pressure to the wound with whatever you have handy; a roller bandage wound firmly up and down the affected limb is best. Seek medical advice immediately.

Bleeding

There are three things to remember in the event of bleeding: pressure, elevate and rest. Whenever I'm chainsawing I keep a roller bandage in my pocket so that I can act immediately in the event of an accident. Be aware

of the dangers and be prepared! I am actually too scared to chainsaw alone. The weekend emergency wards are always overflowing with DIY chainsaw incidents in winter. Don't add to the already heavy burden of the hospitals! Never remove an embedded object, as you can cause as much damage taking it out as it did entering. Get the hospital to remove it. Make sure your tetanus shot is up to date in the event of any cut.

Bruising

Apply ice, if you have any. I only had a freezer after I had finished building, so I never had access to ice. You can also go to the corner store and buy a packet of frozen peas (or an iceblock if you prefer something sweet), then eat it after it's thawed. I received ice from a neighbour once; they happened to be walking by my house as my hand was turning blue and lumpy from the hammer blow it had just received. Handy!

Chemical burns

Rinse under running water for at least 20 minutes. Chemical burns to the eye are treated in the same way, but make sure you run the water *away* from the uninjured eye. Keep doing that for as long as you can stand it, at least 20 minutes. Then see a doctor.

I once splashed acid on my hands, just tiny drops, and didn't rinse it off straightaway as I was too busy and couldn't be bothered to take a break. The next thing I knew, I had festering, painful open wounds wherever the acid had landed, and a slow healing process ahead of me. Don't ignore chemicals! They keep burning for a while, so get rinsing.

Eye injuries

These are very annoying as you will be happily working away one minute, and be in agonizing pain the next. I have cursed myself more times than I can remember for not wearing adequate eye protection, promising that I'll wear glasses the next time…

Never try to remove an embedded or protruding object. Go to hospital! If you can see a *loose* object, moisten a corner of a clean cloth (if all you have is your work shirt, so be it) and gently remove the object. Do not rub your eye as the cornea could get damaged. If the object doesn't come out, rinse your eye with running water. If this also fails, see a doctor.

Falls from roofs, ladders, etc

You'd better hope this doesn't happen to you if you're building alone. If it does, hope you make a loud enough 'thunk' so that someone else will hear and call an ambulance for you.

If you come across someone who has fallen, you might have to move them to facilitate breathing, etc. I really hope you've completed a first aid course, as how to handle an injury this severe can't be adequately explained here.

Heat exhaustion

This can easily occur on a hot day. I used to drink water constantly on site— it was the only way to survive. I think attaching a drip going straight from a backpack to your arm would be a good idea, as then you wouldn't have to think about dehydration. If you feel thirsty, you are already dehydrated. Drink before that happens, and wear a hat in the sun. If you feel giddy, weak or fatigued you are well on your way to heat exhaustion. Move to shade, rest and drink.

If you feel irritable and/or confused, watch out. Passing out with heat stroke could be next. You can *die* from this, as your brain, kidneys and heart amongst other vital organs will begin to fail. Stop what you're doing immediately, rest and have a drink. I was climbing a mountain with a group of students recently, all carrying heavy backpacks. They were dropping like flies! Not enough water and too much exertion. One just stopped walking and started crying; another stood swaying, pale in the face, mumbling, 'I don't feel too well.' Only half an hour ago they'd been happy, strong and buoyant. Heat exhaustion is a fast mover!

Severed fingers, etc

I know a lot of people think you must put a severed finger or other body part on ice. I used to think that too. Please learn that it is *impossible* for a surgeon to reattach a severed finger that has been in direct contact with ice! The ice irrevocably damages the tissue.

Correct procedure is to wrap the finger in a clean cloth, seal it in a plastic bag and then put the bag in a bucket of cold water. If you have ice handy, throw it in the water; it's quite safe.

If you have none of the above, wrap the finger in the cleanest thing you can find and put it in the coolest place you can think of (an air-conditioned car, for example) until you can get the patient to hospital. I would also recommend this course of action if it is your own finger! You are unlikely to want to fiddle around with plastic bags, as you will be trying to deal with your uncontrolled bleeding.

I could say don't work alone in the interests of safety, but I was working alone most of the time. Just be careful and aware and you'll be fine.

Do you want to move in early, shave your legs with warm water from the kettle and wash up in a bucket? I'll show you how it's possible. Plus, you'll learn about good hairdos, how to do a five-minute relaxation, and what to do when friends come over.

In which we learn to cook without a kitchen and get clean without a bathroom!

It's possible for an electrician to wire you up before there's even a house. They can rig up a temporary power point and hey presto, the kettle is whistling. Plumbing is not quite so simple. You can't put in a toilet unless the bathroom is at least vaguely in place. Theoretically, you wouldn't need the rest of the house to be in order, but you would need at least a slab with some temporary walls. Before you move in, you will need to convince your council that you have suitable facilities. There are fines for 'squatting' that your council can impose on you. They can also ask you to move out, with fines being added until you comply.

We had someone call our council, whining about us living illegally on the block. Why anyone would actually care is entirely beyond me. Some people have very small, empty lives which they try to fill to the best of their ability. The truth of the matter was that we were simply spending all our available time on the land, as that was where we wanted to be. We even lived for a while in a friend's garden shed just to save us from paying any more serious rent. We'd go there to sleep and then be back on the land by 6 am the next morning; returning to the friend's shed in the evening before Angus's bedtime, just to stay legal. Anyway, whoever had their binoculars trained on us would see a little light shining at all hours except for late at night, hence the insistent calls to the council. It stressed me immensely, knowing that a hostile person was observing us. I felt stalked. I'd sometimes give a cheery little wave in the direction of the township as a greeting to the mysterious and resentful, self-appointed 'Warden of Temporary Residents'.

Once you have informed the council that you are now living on your property, you will be free to move in properly. It makes things a lot easier when you're living on site, as no time is lost in transit. You can put in an hour after work if you feel like it, and it won't be a big deal since you're already on site. If you have kids, you are around in the afternoon in order to supervise homework. Best of all, because it's still a building site, you don't have to clean the house—just scrape it down occasionally!

COOKING WITHOUT A KITCHEN

My first house didn't have a kitchen. There was a Housing Improvement Order on it due to the lack of cooking facilities, lack of interior doors, crummy wiring, wobbly lean-to and inadequate bathroom. At least I didn't have to worry about ripping out any ugly kitchen fixtures!

We moved in and set up a temporary kitchen housed in the wobbly lean-to using a toaster, a kettle and a borrowed jaffle iron. I was only keen to spend money on things that would bring the house into shape. With a new mortgage, a new baby and a single income (I wasn't working), I wouldn't

even consider buying a microwave oven. Money was really scarce! Secretly I was relieved, as the lack of facilities was the perfect excuse not to cook. Washing up was done in tubs, just like the original owners of the house would have probably done—it was old enough not to have ever had any indoor plumbing.

Food consisted of milk for the baby, gradually moving into jars of baby food; and sandwiches, instant noodles and coffee for the grown-ups. I would make interesting fillings for the jaffle iron; it was quick and easy. Losing that extra pregnancy weight was a piece of cake, as I could no longer bake any delicious treats. My husband ate at work, mostly, so there was only me to cater for. I'd rather have a banana than cook so that was fine. A whole year went by with no changes in the kitchen set-up. I was happy enough at the time, but that was possibly because my brains had been short-circuited due to the child and house arriving almost simultaneously. In retrospect, it seems like unnecessary hardship. I had far superior temporary kitchens later on.

> **Despite being a quick and easy option, takeaways usually have a high fat content and aren't very budget friendly either. However, if you must indulge, go halfway: bake some potatoes in the microwave and buy some takeaway fish to go with them, or pick up a roast chicken and have a homemade salad.**

Kitchen number two, in a different house, was endured for about six months. It consisted of the same reliable toaster, a kettle and a fantastic new addition: a microwave oven. We watched our cholesterol levels plummet as all of the food we ate was steamed, boiled or raw. My fat intake had never been lower.

My best kitchen by far, and one that I can really recommend for any length of time, consisted of the following: a microwave oven, toaster, kettle, toaster oven, gas ring and a small gas bottle. I bought a really attractive two-ringed, stove-top gas burner, and suddenly we could fry things as well! Legally, for indoor use, you can only keep the smallest size of bottle, but this will still last for a long time without needing to be refilled.

With this set-up you need never build a kitchen at all if you don't want to. We lived with this arrangement for three years. The toaster oven will cook cakes, vegetables or whatever you want—except perhaps for whole turkeys, which wouldn't fit. In fact, the only downside is that you no longer have a reason not to cook!

While it's relatively easy to set up a workable cooking arrangement, washing up afterwards is a harder challenge. For a long time we did all the washing up in a bucket. The joy of finally doing the dishes in a sink for the first time in three years and *pulling the plug* afterwards instead of carrying the water outside is hard to describe. Rest assured that you'll learn plenty of one-pot cookery to save on dishes to be washed. It's also good to remember that, however hard you're doing it, historically it was much tougher. Imagine having to start the day by milking the cows and not even being able to refrigerate the milk. Most of us are now blessed with so many mod cons, but it's amazing what you can learn to do without. Even now, with a full kitchen, I sometimes wonder what the point of all that gear is. After all, sometimes all I really need for dinner is a jar of peanut butter and a spoon…

Your temporary kitchen will not have room for all your cooking paraphernalia. Keep only the most needed utensils and only the glasses, plates and so on that you use regularly. Pack the rest away. You will generate less mess and washing-up if you restrict what you keep out. Possibly you will save the family crystal from breaking, too. I kept out six cups, six glasses, four bowls, four plates, a small range of pots and plastic gear, and only the most essential tools. I received a lovely surprise when I unpacked my things later on—my kitchen stuff was in storage for so long that I had forgotten half the things I owned! Because I knew everything was destined for long-term storage, I packed up the old house in two piles: one with all the things that could be damaged by damp and rodents, and the other with those that couldn't be. I did this because we had a rat-and-snake-filled monstrosity called the Scary Shed in the paddock, where we could store most of the stuff. However, the air in it would have been too moist for books and suchlike, so these items were stored elsewhere.

LIVING WITHOUT A PROPER BATHROOM

Your bathroom facilities will have to comply with council rules before it's legal for you to move in. You'll need to provide some form of toilet at the very least—different councils will have different rules. Some rural areas may consider a long drop sufficient; city councils require that you hire a toilet until you can install a permanent one.

Bathroom renovations can be unpleasant. You might have just one bathroom and you don't want it out of commission for long. You might have no bathroom at all; in which case you want to get one happening as soon as possible so you can move in. The bathroom in my first house consisted of a pink bathtub that was propped up on bricks. Orange building plastic surrounded it instead of walls. For a bath mat, you stepped out onto a pallet to keep you off the ground while the plastic flapped around you, sticking to your wet legs. Then the bathtub had to go as a concrete slab was going to be poured where the old bath was. We hired a portaloo on a low monthly rate but had no shower or hot water system. Yet economic constraints demanded we stay put—we couldn't afford to rent as well as pay a mortgage—so we improvized. The only source of water was a garden tap and the hot water service was the kettle.

There might be local gyms or swimming pools you can join for a thorough cleansing. You might have local friends. Give them a bottle of wine for putting up with you. And get that bathroom in fast!

How to heat water without a normal water heater

I am excellent at improvizing hot water, having had a lot of practice! If you have a wood stove it's simple to heat water. Get the stove going and then fill all the pots you own with water and put them on top of it. If you have electricity, there is always the kettle. Two or three kettles mixed with cold water in a big bucket are enough for a not-so frugal wash. In summer you

can use a camping solar shower, which is a flat black bag you leave in the sun to heat. It heats quickly and can easily burn you. Some time ago, I read in the newspaper about some town in New South Wales that had a prolonged power failure. A lot of burns cases were admitted into hospital during this time, as people overheated the water! Another solar-powered way is to buy a coil of black plastic irrigation pipe. Lay it along the ground, fill it with water and leave it to heat in the sun. You can put tap attachments on each side, one to fill and one to drain. In the warmer months, this should be all you need.

HOW TO HOST CELEBRATIONS AND PARTIES

Despite the lack of appropriate facilities, you might want to throw a party at some point, whether for a birthday or for finishing the roof. Gathering a group of pickled people at a building site isn't wise, but I did it anyway. There are a few golden rules you should keep in mind for safety reasons.

Check your building site before your guests arrive. Remove any tripping hazards from the ground, block off where you don't want anyone to wander, and rig up some strong spotlights where people will be walking. You may know exactly where to duck and where to take a big step, but they don't. If you can, plan the party to coincide with a full moon for lots of natural light.

Look out for any situation involving more than one adolescent male. As a group they are prone to endanger themselves and, by doing so, jeopardize you. You don't want to be sued for damages by someone foolish enough to injure himself. If your teenage son wants to host a party, think seriously about the potential hazards on your site because his friends will seek them out.

Casual entertaining

As soon as the slab was poured, we put a big outdoor table in the middle of it, and there it stayed until the house was nearly complete. It could seat a host of people, and provided a venue for informal moonlit gatherings,

workers' lunches and a place to peruse my plans as I worked. Get a big flat door screwed to trestles if you have no table.

The first get-togethers we hosted were either bring-a-plate or pizza. We were only just able to cook for us, not a crowd, and we didn't want to wash up anyway. Be super informal, do finger food. People will understand. If you are the barbecue type of girl, make use of it. Even if you're not, there'll always be a male around willing to show off his prowess at the barbecue!

Formal dining

Formal entertaining is a much harder challenge, particularly when you have to improvise everything, but it's still possible with some determination.

For my husband's birthday one year, I thought a three-course sit-down dinner for 18 would be a good idea. Talk about effort! I had missed entertaining during the kitchen-free period and dislike eating off my lap, so I organized trestle tables, chairs and all the crockery, cutlery and glassware from a function centre. We still had no kitchen on site, so a whole day was spent preparing food, mostly at our temporary home but some in friends' ovens as we didn't have one. We only had a bar fridge, but ice can work wonders in the cooler months. (For a really big do, I'd recommend hiring a towable cool room.) All the washing up was done in a big vat the next day.

Kids' parties

Entertaining groups of kids on a building site can be very scary. What if they fall off things, or into things, like my empty pool? I refused point blank to have any mixed gatherings, where tipsy adults chat whilst the offspring run around outside in the dark. Adults are usually happy for their kids to run free, as they think someone else is keeping an eye on them. There's never enough supervision and it's a situation guaranteed to end in tears. Kids in large mixed groups will not respect your authority as much as they will when it's just you. Depending on how dangerous your site is, however, it can be possible to manage groups of youngsters in dedicated kids' parties.

We certainly had some of those. They were adequately supervized and all ladders leading up to the second floor were removed for safety. For entertaining any large group of young kids, I recommend rigorous planning, just like primary school teachers do. This way, their short attention span is constantly stimulated and mischief is avoided. Plan lots of short games which you can road test first on your own child. For Angus's sixth birthday I had his whole class over. There were no buildings, apart from the cubby and a shed full to the hilt with stuff, so we held the party in the almond grove where the cubby is, and had a big picnic with blankets on the ground. As long as rain stays away a party outdoors is perfect!

Small sleepover parties are very easily held in a tent, and it's extra special for the kids. If it looks like rain put the tent in the carport if you've got one. We had a tent up for a whole month once, serving as a temporary extension and a kid's space. Angus wasn't going to be able to host any sleepovers in his room for a few years, as he didn't have one. His area was a corner of a bigger room, partitioned by bookshelves and cupboards.

When he turned ten, he had a disco. The house was a concrete-floored shell, perfect for any party. These days I would think twice about spilled soft drinks and gluey messes everywhere, but that was a perfect no-fuss setting. We strung twinkling fairy lights overhead, installed a funky friend as a DJ and borrowed a metre of CDs.

Of course, there's always the easy option of hiring a different party location!

11

GIRLIE BITS!

IN WHICH WE EXAMINE THE ISSUES OF HAIR, NAILS, SKIN AND BODY, AND CONSIDER SUITABLE APPAREL FOR BUILDING WORK

This is a topic that concerns some people more than others. If you think vanity is something you throw on a bonfire, skip to a different chapter. My personal vanity comes and goes, but torn builder's shorts can be sexy on a shapely leg all muscled from work...and I'm not just talking about the plumber!

BEAUTY AND HEALTH

As hard to believe as this sounds, your general beauty could actually improve while you build. You will look radiant with happiness as your building takes shape. Odd feelings of pride and joy might surprise you with their power. The journey might be bumpy and you might fall into several low spots along the way, but what you are doing is an amazing achievement and it will show.

Take care of the soul, as it will eventually override everything else. I know, I know, if you are under 25 you may not believe this, but your time will come…

Hair

Do you have tired, lanky, flat hair? Suffer no more, with Premium Cement Root Perm! I'm serious. My hair never looks better than with a bit of cement dust rubbed in it. I swear that's how Farrah Fawcett-Majors did the 'big hair' look in the 1980s. As you mix mortar or concrete, cement dust will fly in the air and your hair will act as a catcher. My hairdresser suggested the root perm analogy, as that's the effect it gives. If on the other hand your hair is big enough without the help of cement, tie it up with a scarf.

After a while I got tired of constantly sweeping hair away from my face, and cut the whole thing off. It felt clean and easy. Now I wear pigtails, for the same reason. Don't bother with hair that needs a lot of styling in order to look good. You might end up having to wash your hair in a bucket with water warmed in the kettle for months on end and suffer serious hat-hair as you either wear a woolly beanie in winter or a sweaty sun hat in the warmer months. Scarves are good for keeping your hair away from your face when the wind blows. Tell your hairdresser you are renovating or building and want something fuss-free. As for me, it's a ponytail, pigtail or plait…except for concreting times when the desire to have big hair gets too strong!

Nails

These will unfortunately go. You won't mean for it to happen, but one by one they will break. By the time you have broken the third one you will come

to the realization that nails are no longer for you. On a positive note, as a builder, you won't have to file or cut your nails as this automatically gets done for you.

The last time I visited my family for an extended period of time I noticed to my surprise that my nails were growing. This hadn't happened in a very long time, as only restful activities will bring on the nails. I got all excited and started making exaggerated hand gestures, pretending to be a sales person on the perfume counter.

I'm looking at my nails as I write. There was a time when I cared for them. I filed and polished. They were never very long but there was hope. Then I did the only sensible thing and gave up. There are other things you can do to be glamorous, but I remember the nice feeling of slender, well cared for fingers complete with nails. That was a long time ago…

Hands

Oh dear. I hope you aren't too fussy about the state of your hands. I love how mine look now; they show I am capable of doing things. They also show significant wear. As a bonus, I will never be asked to work on the perfume counter selling hand cream. By the way, if that is your job and you are planning to start a new hobby building, you might have to change career.

Avoid wearing rings, as you might damage them and they will become filled with dirt. The same goes for most jewellery. I have been known to wear pearls but only for light work.

There is a glove for every occasion. Wear gloves if you like but I often don't bother as I feel direct contact gives me more control.

Skin

Ensure you drink enough water! Your lips will crack and dry out if you don't, and your skin will feel like paper. Wear sun screen, even when it's not summer. I'm very bad with this and will probably end up having to surgically

reconstruct my skin in a few years time. Have you ever noticed the road workers with their crocodile necks? Aren't they the best advertisement for wearing hats with brims that you ever saw?

Wear sunglasses to prevent squinting. Where I live it's so jolly bright most of the time that squinting is unavoidable as soon as you step outside the door. Oh for the dull low light of northern Europe…

Body

If you are doing some of the physical things on site you will be amply rewarded. Over the course of a two-week holiday I was insanely busy laying bricks in my two-storey gables. To reach the apex, I had to climb two sets of ladders resting on a little platform halfway up. I could carry one big brick each climb. Then I would climb up with a metal bucket dangling against my legs, bruising me as I went, that contained enough mortar to lay a couple of bricks. Plastic buckets don't keep their shape when filled with something as heavy as mortar! Towards the end of my holiday I happened to catch sight of myself in the mirror, and the side of my torso was *rippling*! Unfortunately, musculature not maintained will quickly dwindle.

When you observe some builders, and see their gut and generally unfit appearance, you might wonder how physical their work really is. Of course, they often have apprentices and lackeys who do the hard stuff. The boss stays on the ground calling the shots, then tucks into a couple of meat pies followed by some beers after work. Uncharitable? You look for yourself. Not all of them are like that of course, but there are enough around to discern a pattern. One of the best examples of lean, muscly and fit men I have ever seen was one of my concreters. He spent large parts of his day swinging a pickaxe into compacted clay in 40°C (104°F) heat, uncomplaining. He had no apprentice. That's one way to get a truly brilliant physique.

Health

To get the most pleasure and least pain from your project, good health is essential. You already know all the stuff about eating right and getting

exercise; now's the time to put it into practice. You will be getting plenty of exercise as you work, but you'll need a higher than normal calorie intake to sustain yourself. Ensure you get enough protein to build muscle.

Take care to stop occasionally, especially if you feel sick or things will get worse. I worked right through flu and got pneumonia instead. Watch out! Also, as you work it is a good idea to have high and low jobs to avoid back injuries. If you work bent over today, work stretched high tomorrow. Warm up at the start of each day by doing five minutes of stretches. You don't want to strain yourself. If your legs, arms and stomach are strong, you are less likely to lift with your back.

I swear by chocolate for when you run really short of energy and need a fast pick-me-up. Make sure you always have some in the house!

You only truly appreciate good health when it's gone. Enjoy it now, and do all you can to keep it.

CLOTHES

This is the sad part of building. You will, quite possibly, end up looking awful and getting so used to it you won't mind going to the shops dressed like a hobo. My husband surprised me by hating it when I went shopping in my work gear. As far as I was concerned, I would waste precious time if I got changed just to go down the road. I didn't think such a petty thing would bother him.

At the very least, your working wardrobe should consist of a couple of T-shirts, one jumper, one shirt, a pair of shorts, a pair of pants, a woolly hat, a sun hat, work socks and work boots. Don't think you can wear your ordinary clothes and not damage them. That's only possible on television! I have sections of my wardrobe dedicated to different degrees of dirty work. There are clothes that I don't like so much and these are kept for really rough work. Other clothes are worn for jobs like carpentry, as you don't get so dirty. For really messy things like tiling, you will probably need to throw the clothes out after you have finished, so it's a good idea to pick up some clothes from an op shop if you haven't got anything you want to discard. Tiling tends to put

glue and grout on your hands, and as you'll then wipe your hands on your pants (even though there's a perfectly good rag handy), you'll find your pants build up so much stuff on them they can stand independently of you afterwards. You can't put them in the washing machine, as the glue and grout will clog up the pipes. Just throw the clothes out!

You can, of course, shop specially for building gear. As you will spend hours in these clothes, make sure they are comfy and that you like wearing them. Perhaps a stylish set of Hard Yakkas is just the ticket? Flannelette shirts have a certain look, and provide warmth. I used to own one, especially acquired for building work, but my electric planer ate it.

Shoes are important, too. I have a couple of different pairs for building. If you are going to work with stone I recommend steel cap boots (you *will* drop rocks), otherwise anything that has a covered toe for safety will do. Thongs won't do! I adore elastic-sided boots, and have three pairs. One pair for building (but I also build in a pair of bright blue Doc Martens), and two more slimline, higher quality pairs for leisure wear.

I'm sure you can think up some interesting outfits. You will wear them day in and day out for a very long time, so make sure you like them! However, if you decide to wear your favourite stuff, brace yourself for that first tear or indelible stain. After that it doesn't matter.

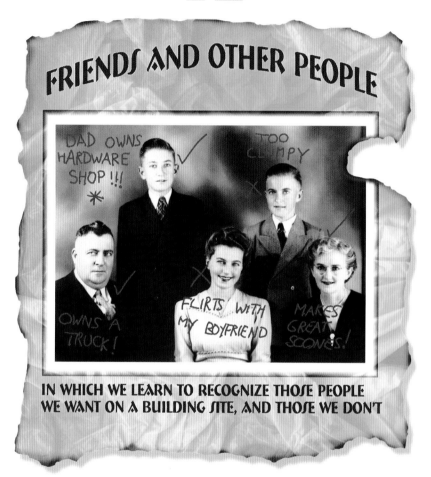

12

FRIENDS AND OTHER PEOPLE

IN WHICH WE LEARN TO RECOGNIZE THOSE PEOPLE WE WANT ON A BUILDING SITE, AND THOSE WE DON'T

If someone tells you something isn't possible, it doesn't necessarily mean they're right. It may mean *they* can't do it, or they think you shouldn't do it for whatever reason. These people may often be your friends with what they see as your best interests at heart. It can be very hard not to listen to them. Don't worry, the same people will come back in a couple of years time and say 'you're so lucky' when they see what you've accomplished. Lucky? Bloody hardworking is more like it!

CRITICS AND DETRACTORS

Your biggest critic may in fact be yourself. Stop it. There are enough people willing to put you down already; you don't need to add to the list. Some older Aussie men are still of the opinion that women have no place drinking in pubs, let alone touching tools. Understand that these men exist, and that you can't change them. Let them be. Indulge them in their little ways. Some men are sadly stuck in the demanding role of living up to other men. Overtake one of these men when you are driving and you have effectively emasculated him. Imagine what you are doing to him if you overtake him in a traditionally male dominated area such as building!

I once overheard a boorish man call me 'a weird f***ing builder chick'. He is very macho and works with heavy machinery. Oh well, I'm obviously not his type. Do I need to add he's not mine either?

A couple of years ago I had a pet dislike. At the time, I was really struggling, working myself to such exhaustion I once or twice fell asleep at night fully dressed and coated with dirt. Friends would come to visit—rested, clean and refreshed kind of people. They would brush the dirt from the chairs before sitting down, look around and cheerfully tell me things like the following:

- If I lived here I would… finish that/weed this/build a laundry/install a wind-powered power plant.

- You should… pave this/paint that/line the driveway in oak trees interspersed with Moravian pansies.

- Why don't you… grow another set of arms/earn more money/create 50 extra hours in the week?

I couldn't cope with these comments. I could only barely cope with the task at hand. At that point I was so very tired of the whole thing. I had to prioritize, and so I let waist-high weeds grow unchecked in order to do things that I found actually mattered. I needed to focus on small chunks that I could handle. Having well-meaning people lay more work, mentally, on you can be the proverbial 'straw that broke the camel's back'.

Some people can't keep their opinions to themself. 'Surely that blue is not the final colour?' was an interesting comment from a friend on seeing my colour choice for the woodwork. Well, I saw her house and thought it hideously 1970s, but I would never dream of commenting adversely on her decorating skills. (I will only think it, instead!)

'Is that finished?' was another great comment. Some folk are very insensitive. I believe you are allowed to slap them with a laden paintbrush if they make such comments more than once.

People often feel the need to tell you what you should do. 'Why don't you just pay someone to finish it for you?' was hard to deal with as I replied through gritted teeth, 'I have no money'. 'Just borrow some', was usually the response. I didn't want to! Many people will not understand if you have chosen to build slowly with cash instead of using borrowed money at a high rate of interest. If you want to go down the rather difficult route of not borrowing, assuming of course that you have some prospect of an income and have a decent sum saved already, be assured that *it is possible to do.*

Bear in mind that some people thrive on finding faults in others. I think it makes them feel better about themselves. If you encounter that sort of person, you will have to switch off. It isn't worth arguing with them. Instead, walk away.

All houses will have some shortcomings. Yours will too. You don't have to make excuses for the things that are less than perfect. I take everything personally: plants that die are my fault, flaky paint is my fault. I'm also to blame for any warped timber or rusty metal. I don't take criticism very well but I'm learning.

My biggest mistake is a leaning doorway. When I first erected it, it was as straight as anything. Then, my mistake began. I started bricking up one side of the wall only, and without my noticing it, each course of the wall pushed the doorframe ever so slowly out of true. When I finally noticed, the whole wall was complete and I decided to ignore it, as I didn't want to demolish all those weeks of work. Anyway, the old houses of Europe lean, and maybe my

house was trying to be like them… But the amount of people who've commented on it!

'Did you know that doorframe is crooked?'

'Really? No! Thanks for pointing it out to me; I'll get right on it.'

I got so sick of it I nearly bricked the whole thing up just to shut everyone up. I would be lying if I said I didn't care, and I still haven't resolved what to do with it. I might eventually hang a curtain over the door so I don't have to talk to people about it. At the moment there are some planks leaning over it; they detract from the whole crooked issue as they lean in another direction. Possibly I'll get over it in time and it will be the biggest attraction of the whole house. Not every house has a door as wonky as mine. Now people who haven't noticed and who like other people's mistakes will check it out when they visit. I should have kept it to myself!

There are people who will actually believe you have finally flipped, and though they may not tell you so to your face, they will possibly talk with others. You can find yourself becoming an oddity. I used to excitedly talk about my house-building interest, but stopped when I realized it was seen as a little peculiar.

It's amazing how all that has changed these days. I'm being taken seriously! You have to laugh.

UNSEEN ENEMIES

While I'm on the subject of less than desirable people, I might as well deal with those who steal from building sites. This is a sad fact of life, but there are a few precautions you can take to minimize losses.

- If materials are being delivered, try to arrange for them to arrive when someone is at home. If you work full time, this is hard, but take the afternoon off, rather than risk losing your supplies—especially the more expensive things like hot water units and other plumbing gear. Your insurance is unlikely to cover those things.

- Don't leave *anything* by the kerb; some people see it as free to take.

- Have fences put up as a priority.

- Don't leave stuff in the house until you have a locking front door. My car boot was a mobile toolbox that never got unpacked, but I would have been very unhappy if I'd lost the car!

- Get to know your neighbours. Perhaps they will help keep an eye out for any unusual activity around your site. Then again, they might not! A couple of times I have been invited to collect brick leftovers from people I barely knew. Their builders had finished and had left the odd half pallet of bricks that needing cleaning up. So, armed with the address and a borrowed trailer, I have gone in broad daylight and simply loaded up without anyone bothering me. A lot of suburbs are sleeping ones only with few people around during the day. The crime rate is especially high, I believe, in new housing estates where many people are building but few have moved in.

- And finally, you are less likely to lose things if you are living on site, so move in as quickly as you can.

KEEPING YOUR FRIENDS

One of the problems with building is that you can be too busy to socialize. Where's the time for friends when all your spare time is taken up with the house? Life goes on, one month flows into the next and *still* you don't see them. Sometimes you don't even get to talk on the phone. I didn't have a phone for a while, and when I finally did, I was never near enough to hear the rings. I said that if anyone needed me urgently I would be close to the phone between 4.15 and 4.30 pm each day; other than that, they had to try me after 9 pm. Eventually, I bought a cordless phone so I could carry it around with me. These days I even have a mobile, which I couldn't afford back when I needed it.

If you have entertained the idea of inviting your friends over to work with you, be careful. They will probably come once or twice until the novelty

wears off. After that they will avoid you. Only ask them if there is something too big for you to handle yourself. I have asked people over in order to lift lintels into place, raise windows, lift ceiling roses, move a rainwater tank into place (that took over a dozen of the very kindest sort of people), and such like. Take care not to wear your helpers out or next time they'll have a better excuse: 'The hernia hasn't healed yet!'

When you do finally manage to socialize, beware of the boredom trap! For the non-builder or renovator, it is hideously boring to listen to endless chatter about floor-finishes and the choices of sandpaper grit available. It is second only to the new parents going on about how cute their baby is. I'm sure it's cute, but it's a very boring topic for the people not involved. If you see people's eyes start to glaze over, change the subject. This requires you to switch from the topic foremost in your head and pull out another one. It can be hard, I know. What ever did you talk about prior to renovating or building? Look forward to those rare times when you will find yourself talking to someone with a similar building obsession. Then you can enthuse to each other about 'hammers I have used' or 'the long-term effect of polyurethane on Baltic pine' for as long as you like!

I still have my friends. They accepted that I wouldn't come to many daytime gatherings as that took away daylight building hours. They learnt that I was usually only available after 6 pm at the earliest. And when I finally showed up I learnt to talk about growing freesias, the contemporary scarcity of myxomatosis and why the government milk subsidy isn't greater…anything but building!

PICKING UP GUYS

If you have all the friends you need, but half fancy a new partner as you lost the last one due to building arguments, this section is for you.

Based on personal experience, I am in two minds as to how much you tell people you've just met about yourself. Men can feel threatened by you if you seem briskly competent in a traditionally male area. Don't ask me why,

they're just like that. If you are competent in floral arrangement, they won't bat an eyelid. They can also be worried by power, so be careful if you are the CEO of a mining company, for instance.

Below is a snippet of conversation that clearly illustrates some of the pitfalls you may encounter.

> **Dishy Man:** And what do you do in your spare time?
>
> **You, looking sweet and demure:** I'm at the moment utterly obsessed by single-handedly building my very own stone copy of Chartres Cathedral. And you?'
>
> (Man walks away, deflated, thinking you're not his type.)

Let's try that again:

> **Dishy Man:** And what do get up to on the weekend?
>
> **You, looking sweet and demure:** I like shopping [*for hardware*], you know, barbecues [*making them*], friends [*having them over to help*], maybe some horse riding. And you?
>
> **Man, still very dishy:** Yeah, same, you know. Want to go out for dinner sometime?

Remember that developing a new relationship takes dedicated time and effort. Do you really have the time? Do you want to make the time? You may prefer finishing the tiling to dating now, but it's nice to have someone to admire the tiles when you're done.

Then, when you are at the romantic dinner for two, you can tell him about your unusual hobby if you wish. Once I went to a dinner date with blue-spattered paint stains on my shins and hands that just wouldn't come off, prompting the question of exactly what I was doing in my spare time. Allow him the room to surprise you with interests you never expected. Perhaps he enjoys having pretend conversations with his teddies (this sounds promising!) or visiting the housebound with library books and his special

homemade oaten biscuits. There are unexpected depths to many people, but you could scare some potential suitors off by coming on too strong with the house stuff… I can hardly believe I'm saying all this but it's *true*. I'm sure you have many other things to talk about as well. Anyway, discussing building *is* boring.

When I first arrived in Australia I was amazed at the way guys opened doors for me and paid for drinks. Chivalry was still alive, which is more than could be said for Sweden. The drawback, of course, is that Australian men expect their women to be well, women! What I'm about to say may not apply to all men, but it does to a fair few: men appear to worry that a woman will turn into a man if she shows an interest in building.

Why this is so, I'm just not sure. Do *you* feel threatened if a man holds a frying pan in his hand? Of course not! I melt with desire, wondering what delectable treats he might be able to cook for dinner. Why does a man find a woman with a hammer in her hand threatening? Does he think she'll hit him with it? Of course, if you are a man reading this, and you find a woman builder appealing instead of a threat, then I thank you.

Women can find it difficult to understand you, too! I once had a female friend tell me in all seriousness to 'wear pink more often' as it would help me to attract the kind of man who could take over the work. Oh yeah? Did she ever consider that I actually enjoyed doing the building myself? It's certainly the best hobby I've had so far. I want to be a girl *without* the pink and *with* the hammer. And if you do too, then don't let anyone stop you!

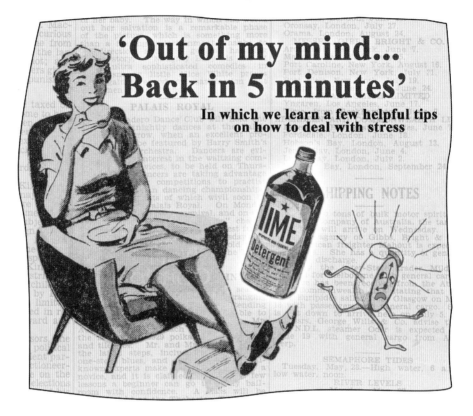

13

'Out of my mind... Back in 5 minutes'

In which we learn a few helpful tips on how to deal with stress

I don't bite my nails, but I get going on the skin on my knuckles whenever agitation sets in. And the cuticles! Yes, I confess I get so stressed that I resort to a bit of self-mutilation. A little bit of stress is great—it will raise the blood pressure and make things more up-tempo—but it can be very damaging, both physically and mentally, if the levels rise too much. It pays to remember that there's no point in worrying about things that haven't happened yet. You'll have plenty of real worries to focus on if you're working on a house, anyway. I always have a bag full, and while I try to take that bag out with the rubbish every week, it often hangs around.

STRESS-BUSTING TIPS

Are you easily stressed by change? Change is going to be a way of life for a while if you decide to build or renovate, so you need to develop some skills to help you deal with the accompanying stress.

It helps to plan ahead, but try not to be too concerned when things don't work out the way you thought they would. Expect the unexpected. Perhaps your initial plan wasn't that good anyway. Make alternative plans to suit the new turn of events.

If it stresses you when things don't turn out *your* way, you will end up in a state of perpetual anxiety. Instead, stand back and take a look at your situation from a different vantage point. Ask yourself some questions. If you like, write down the answers in order to look at them more objectively. These questions might not be the right ones for every occasion but I'm sure you can think of plenty more yourself.

I find vitamin B really helps me if I'm stressed. A two-week course works wonders. Maybe I'm imagining things but I suggest you try for yourself.

- What exactly happened?

- Why did it happen?

- Was it within my control or was it due to outside forces?

- Can I reverse it, and would that be a good thing?

- If I can't reverse it, can I live with it?

There are some other useful techniques that will help you to regain control of the new, altered situation.

- Don't overdramatize matters.

- Refrain from talking to negative people too often and mentally prepare responses to their comments beforehand.

- Take a short break occasionally. Whenever I went anywhere, even to the

shops, I would feel invisible strings pulling me back on site. But it's a good idea to remove yourself sometimes in order to regain perspective. And with perspective comes control.

◆ Don't feel you must be completely competent and never make any mistakes; it'll hurt more when you fall!

The power of 'should' and 'could'

Some time ago I learnt a very interesting little technique that I try to apply to my life as much as possible. Use the word 'could' instead of 'should'. It sounds much better. Try this exercise:

> This weekend I should second-coat the skirtings, stop the gutter leaking, and drive young Winston to tennis before having dinner with the Fendhursts.

Now rephrase the sentence like this:

> This weekend I could second-coat the skirtings, stop the gutter leaking, and drive young Winston to tennis before having dinner with the Fendhursts.

…if I feel like it!

You heap loads of guilt on yourself by imposing all those 'shoulds' on your life. A shift to 'could' changed the way I look at things. Similarly, other people have a loathsome habit of knowing what's best for you: 'You should do this, you should do that'. Get into the habit of *never* starting a sentence with 'you should'. People will be more receptive if you begin with 'you could'.

SEIZE THE DAY

Good time management should help to free some up for you, not be the cause of more stress.

Time is your wealth, your most important non-renewable resource. You might have someone good with finances to manage those, but how do you

manage your time, which is so much more valuable? These days we all imagine we are short of time. A couple of generations ago, my grandparents appeared to have all the time in the world. Where did all their time come from, when I seem to have so little? I admit to being divided here; one part of me says let time happen and another says grab it, this is a moment you'll never see again. I think that as I mature I will be more amenable to letting time run at its own pace.

You probably know your disposable income, but do you know your disposable time? Whatever time is going spare, you can use on your house. Sometimes you will struggle to find enough time. I know I do. What are you spending your time on at the moment? Something will have to go if your week is already full. One of my big time fillers is lying down and having a good long read, with a block of hazelnut chocolate for company. But this doesn't achieve anything. Or does it? Perhaps it rests me in readiness for further exertion.

Time is yours to spend—use it wisely. While you will go mad sometimes and frivolously waste some, on the whole you will need to be quite disciplined.

Do you ferry children to sport? Do you have to, or can they go by bike or get driven by someone else? Could you afford to take some time off work? Regrettably, you will need all the money you can find, so you need to find a balance that is workable. After my first year of building, I started taking one day off a week. That was all I could afford, but it worked marvels by giving me blocks of undisturbed time in which to get things done. My Tuesdays were truly magical. I would plan them beforehand so no time would be wasted, and they would flow as smoothly as possible. A friend of mine who is an opera singer would come by and rehearse her music, as my house was a good acoustic space, so I would work away to the sound of live opera. I loved it; it felt like I was a character in an Italian movie.

Time and the television

We used to have the television in a separate little building 100 metres (330 feet) from the house. It was great. To avoid unnecessary trips we would

read the television guide first and plan our viewing. After separating from my husband I didn't have a television at all for over a year as I gladly let him keep it. (You'd be surprised at how little you miss television when you don't have any access to it!) Then someone offered me one complete with a VCR and six creaky dining chairs in exchange for one of my paintings. I accepted, and now my son watches far too much television and I watch sparingly. There is so much else to do!

Television is a big thief of available hours. Perhaps there is only one program you want to watch, but after it ends you stay sitting there in front of the box. Soon the evening's over. If you are an addictive watcher, resist the temptation to even switch the television on. Once you are hooked on watching a series it is hard to break the habit. If you must see it, record it and watch it at the end of the evening.

Make every hour count

After work each day, I found there were never enough daylight hours to build much, especially in the darker months. Instead I would come home, have coffee, get changed, and then carry bricks around the site. I would stack bricks on the walls ready for the weekend's laying and prepare whatever else I could. Only then would I go inside to make dinner. This way, the building zoomed along at weekends as all the backbreaking preparation work had been done during the week.

If you put in one extra hour a day, you gain a whole seven-hour day each week! After dinner, is there anything you can do indoors? An hour or two a day makes a big difference and you'll hardly notice it. A favourite pastime of mine that filled in many long dark evenings is leadlight. I could do it whatever the weather, and it made me feel like I was progressing if I did something every day.

Keep lists, make notes

A scrap of wood is a good thing to write a shopping list on as you won't easily lose it, and it won't blow away on site. The builders all do it! Write

down things you need from the hardware as you think of them, so you won't forget them later. It's awful going to the hardware three times in a day because of bad planning.

Write lists of the jobs that need doing, what you need to do them, and how much you think it's going to cost. Make sure there are always a couple of different jobs on the go, and it's good if one of them is something you can stop-start. By that I mean something that doesn't require mixing anything that will set if not used immediately, and something that won't need mountains of cleaning up afterwards.

Make notes in your diary, just brief ones outlining what you did: on Monday I planted two walnut trees, and painted the laundry door; on Tuesday I laid a lintel; on Wednesday I hung the back gate. Then, when you are tired and feel nothing is progressing, you can read back over a few months and realize what you've accomplished. I'm amazed sometimes that I couldn't see the progress for myself; it was too gradual. A bit of positive retrospection is always great for your enthusiasm.

You have to feed yourself and any kids you might have, but that takes time. Far too much time gets wasted on shopping and cooking already, so why not cook double portions and freeze half?

Be generous with schedules

Don't set unrealistic deadlines for jobs; be generous with time. The trades tend to be unrealistic all the time, and regrettably, they often miscalculate. You wonder how they can calculate the material needed if they can't calculate the time.

I'd write some notes on my calendar, but that was more to act as a guideline than a strict goal. After all, as a novice you can't possibly know how long anything is going to take. A greater concern for me was how much money I would have when, as the planned jobs had to fit in with that. I would work out a savings plan, and know when I could order what.

Hobbies and socializing

Do you play any sport? Sorry, you'll have to shelve that for now. The team will just have to wait for you. Better still; invite the team over to help you for a day! Sport takes a lot of time. You have weeknight practice, weekend games, fundraisers and socials. Other hobbies will also have to take a back seat, just for a little while. You will now have no time for *anything* on the weekend apart from your project. Only on television do renovations and whole buildings happen over a couple of days.

You will have less time for everything. You might not see your friends as much, but there are ways you can get round this. A friend of mine knows how bad I feel if I spend too much time socializing, so when she comes to stay for the weekend she brings jeans and a hammer. If she works with me for a few hours, I have saved myself that time and can relax in her company.

Another friend, also a single mother, would do dinner exchanges with me at least once a week. I would cook for her family and mine, and then she would reciprocate. It was very casual, saved time on cooking and also got some socializing in. It was lovely for us and great fun for the kids.

In short, you'll have to give things up or find time where previously there was none. Catch time as it goes by—or it will go 'bye!'

RELAXATION

There is no doubt relaxing is beneficial to us. You will sleep better, think better, be better equipped to cope with unpleasant surprises, feel happier and be more at ease with yourself. For your benefit, I have outlined a quick five-or-so minute relaxation technique, although you could take as much time as you want for the middle section. Do you have 20 minutes to spare? Go ahead and invest it in a lie-down. As W.H. Davies said in 'Leisure' in 1911:

What is this life if, full of care,
We have no time to stand and stare?

1. Find a comfy spot; remove anything obstructive like glasses or shoes. At my building site/home the comfiest place used to be the front seat of my car. It offered a cosy, uninterrupted, upholstered bit of privacy. It even had an adjustable back and personal heating!

2. Close your eyes and focus on your breathing. Relax your body and let it sink heavily into the seat. Feel your weight. Listen to any sounds outside and inside your cocoon. Be aware of the presence of sound but don't let it worry you. Cars passing, birds chirping, someone running…

3. When ready, take a deep breath, starting far down in your stomach. I sometimes imagine my breath travelling up and down like an elevator rising and falling. Slowly exhale through your mouth. Feel your body relax more deeply as you continue focusing on your breathing. Count to four as you inhale, four as you exhale. Do this about three times, as too much can make you light-headed. Then return to normal breathing.

4. Now you can do some visualization if you like. I sometimes imagine a powerful shaft of bright golden energizing light travelling through me as I simply continue breathing. You might prefer to picture a tranquil place where you can linger for a few minutes. You could gently repeat a word or mantra that has meaning for you. Perhaps you could picture yourself doing that tricky thing you were about to tackle, and look: there you are, doing it in a perfectly calm and competent manner. It doesn't even look hard! Alternatively, why not see yourself standing tall, feeling fit, strong and healthy as the sun shines on your face and a light breeze blows in your hair? Maybe you are standing triumphantly on top of the roof, the building beneath you all finished and looking great.

5. As you prepare to re-open your eyes, talk kindly to yourself about your coming tasks. Be supportive and encouraging—someone has to be!

6. Slowly open your eyes, sit up and move into the rest of the day.

Do this as often as you like. It will help to prevent stress as well as reduce it.

14

After my win with *Better Homes and Gardens* I had a lot of unexpected publicity. The publicity, in turn, generated much response from all kinds of people, but mostly women. It was tremendously exciting to see the reaction people had. I was a bit embarrassed, really, but hugely flattered as well.

All the women who approached me, saying they wished they could do what I had done, are the reason I wrote this book. They said I made it seem so easy that they just might give it a try. Did I have any advice to give them? Well, I happened to have quite a lot. So much, it filled a whole book! I could have kept going, but everyone has to stop somewhere…

Perhaps you dream of some day starting on something exciting, with or without a partner. Be assured that though it is hard work, it's not really all that difficult. The world needs more inspired women, putting their feminine skills to good use. Hopefully I have managed to convey the message that *you* can be such a woman. I truly believe every woman can, and if I have managed to inspire you with this book, my work is done.

I love the company of men, and appreciate their strength and ability, but I don't need them around any more to fix things or make stuff. I have discovered that I can do it myself!

Despite all the messy drawbacks, I love building. It is the single most exciting thing I have ever done with the exception of becoming a parent. It is a laborious, exhausting but incredibly fulfilling journey of love, from the planning and building to surviving its many challenges. There is potential for unlimited excitement as you realize your dreams. Life's full of possibilities, go for it!

Some day when the cornices are finally up I might think about plotting out another house, but until then, I'll leave you to the excitement of drawing your own plans… You can look forward to the moment when you stand back, admire your project and know that it was built like a woman.

index

Published in 2004 by Murdoch Books®, a division of Murdoch Magazines Pty Ltd.

Murdoch Books Australia®
Pier 8/9
23 Hickson Road
Sydney NSW 2000
Phone: +61 (02) 8220 2000
Fax: +61 (02) 8220 2558

Murdoch Books UK Ltd
Erico House, 6th Floor North
93/99 Upper Richmond Road
Putney London SW15 2TG
Phone: +44 (0) 20 8785 5995
Fax: + 44 (0) 20 8785 5985

Chief Executive: Juliet Rogers
Publisher: Kay Scarlett

Editor: Anouska Jones
Designer: Jacqueline Duncan
Editorial Director: Diana Hill
Creative Director: Marylouise Brammer
Production: Monika Vidovic

National Library of Australia Cataloguing-in-Publication Data
Broman, Sandra. Built like a woman. Includes index. ISBN 1 74045 390 5. 1. Dwellings - Maintenance and repair - Amateurs' manuals. 2. Dwellings - Remodeling - Amateurs' manuals. I. Title

Printed by Sing Cheong Printing Co. Ltd. PRINTED IN HONG KONG.

ACKNOWLEDGEMENTS
Thanks to Pauline Jeske for saying, 'You must enter this competition'; Ian Marden for saying, 'Why don't you write a book?'; Roff Smith, my mentor Fenely Bygg, Fran Moore, Diana Hill, Anouska Jones, Jacqueline Duncan, Kay Scarlett and Juliet Rogers for making it happen; and finally the supremely marvellous Richard Baxter for everything else.

NOTES:
You will find I have used the word 'he' when talking about tradespeople. To write 'he/she' everywhere is so very messy! I also have yet to meet a female tradesperson, and would love to see more skilled females out there!